Solzhenitsyn's

One Day in the Life of Ivan Denisovich

Robert Porter

Bristol Classical Press

Critical Studies in Russian Literature

First published in 1997 by
Bristol Classical Press
an imprint of
Gerald Duckworth & Co. Ltd
The Old Piano Factory
48 Hoxton Square, London N1 6PB

A catalogue record for this book is available
from the British Library

ISBN 1-85399-470-7

Available in USA and Canada from:
Focus Information Group
PO Box 369
Newburyport
MA 01950

Printed in Great Britain by
Booksprint, Bristol

Contents

Preface

We need to rehearse some arguments for adding to the already voluminous writings about Solzhenitsyn. *One Day in the Life of Ivan Denisovich* remains Solzhenitsyn's most famous work, even now, nearly thirty-five years since its first publication, and after a literary achievement that currently runs to more than two dozen hefty volumes in a forthcoming *Collected Works*. This short novel (it is designated a *povest'*) features regularly in university syllabuses, and is a work that students respond to enthusiastically and are keen to write essays on.

Yet, in my experience, the essays all too often fall short of the enthusiasm that drives them; and students are unable or unwilling to venture beyond a reiteration of Solzhenitsyn's talent and courage – moral and physical – in exposing the iniquities of Stalinism. There must be more to the story than factual exposure, especially since the work endures still, even though the political system which it challenged so effectively has disappeared. One could argue that part of the Western reader's inability to articulate a sophisticated response lies in the 'Russianness' of the work. If this were so, a good many other Russian works of fiction would likewise suffer at the hands of apprentice literary critics in the West. Yet 'difficult' and very 'Russian' authors (Gogol, Bulgakov and, of course, Pushkin) never fail to produce at least *some* good criticism at undergraduate level.

A more likely explanation is perhaps to be found in the English translations of the work. *Ivan Denisovich* is linguistically an extremely demanding text and even those who have mastered standard Russian find themselves resorting to English-language versions. As I have sought to demonstrate in Chapter One, the most readily available English translation for many years, that by Ralph Parker, is woefully inadequate, and the early attempts by others also leave a lot to be desired. Harry Willetts' version, the authorised translation, is a magnificent feat and will doubtless do much to improve the general reader's appreciation of the novel's power. But a translation can do only so much. Our reading of the text in Part Two is designed to illustrate that the original urges the reader towards notions beyond the purely political and factual, while never losing sight of these. Our reading makes no claims to being definitive, and it is intended to offer suggestions rather than to pontificate. Its lacunae and deficiencies may so incense Solzhenitsyn fans that – by default as it were – it will fulfil its aim and stimulate more subtle and more closely argued literary criticism.

As endnoted in Part Two, the translations of quotations from *Ivan Denisovich* are my own and are intended primarily to show how the Russian original 'works'. Quotations from some other works (notably, *The Calf Butted the Oak* [English published title *The Calf and the Oak*], *The First Circle*) are my own. I have, however, used the widely available English translations for quotations from some peripheral sources and from *The Gulag Archipelago*, referring the reader to the corresponding passage in the original, and commenting, where appropriate, on any discrepancies.

I would like to express my gratitude to Michael Nicholson for putting his extraordinary expertise in all matters relating to Solzhenitsyn repeatedly at my disposal and for his careful reading of the draft version of this book. His comments, knowledge of source materials and good sense have helped me no end in reducing the number of factual errors and in refining my own judgments. These latter do not always coincide with his, and my obduracy and obtusity cry out for his indulgence and that of my readers. The series editor, Neil Cornwell, also deserves thanks for his discriminating reading of the text and for his suggestions for its improvement. I should also like to thank Birgit Beumers for tracking down details relating to Lev Grossman and Yuri Zavadsky for me.

Robert Porter
Bristol 1996

A Note on Transliteration

In the body of the text I have tried to be reasonably consistent without being pedantic in transliterating Cyrillic, using the now widely accepted versions of certain proper nouns, surnames and the like (e.g. *Literaturnaya gazeta*, *Novy mir*, Dostoevsky) in preference to forms demanded by any rigidly applied transliteration scheme. However, in the Notes, Bibliography and wherever I have felt that precision is important, notably in supplying the original of particular quotations, I have used the Library of Congress system.

If we except those miraculous and isolated moments fate can bestow on a man, loving your work (unfortunately the privilege of a few) represents the best, the most concrete approximation of happiness on earth. But this is a truth that not many know. [...] We can and must fight to see that the fruit of labor remains in the hands of those who work, and that work does not turn into punishment; but love, or conversely, hatred of work is an inner, original heritage, which depends greatly on the story of the individual and less than is believed on the productive structures within which the work is done.

(*The Wrench*, Primo Levi, translated by William Weaver, Abacus, 1986, pp. 79-80)

Part One

Introduction
The Story of a Book's Publication

'He never shares anything with anyone; he is a fully quali-
fied, resourceful and merciless jackal; he is a total egoist,
living only for his belly. [...] He is a real traitor to his country.'

'Although I wept when I read it, I felt myself a citizen with
full rights among other people. Up till then I felt their chilly
glances and they reminded me of Pechora and Norilsk.'[1]

Has there ever been a book in modern times, in an age when literature has
to compete fiercely with all other media, that has generated so much
controversy and has shaken a seemingly invincible government so pro-
foundly as *One Day in the Life of Ivan Denisovich*? The reactions quoted
above to the book (henceforth referred to as *Ivan Denisovich*) from two
Soviet readers illustrate not just the divergence of views Solzhenitsyn's text
produced but also the sheer *power* that it possesses. In the storm that broke
on its publication in November 1962, the political and historical questions
that it raised naturally overshadowed the subtler aesthetic qualities that the
work had, though time and again readers and reviewers made reference to
the graphic qualities of the work, to its authenticity. The author's ability
to convey a sense of reality even led to a pun: *Solzhenitsyn ne solzhët*
(Solzhenitsyn will not tell a lie).[2] The publication of *Ivan Denisovich* has
come to stand as one of the major landmarks in Russian literary history. It
was quite natural for Geoffrey Hosking to subtitle *Beyond Socialist Realism*,
his survey of Russian literature of the 1960s and 70s, 'Soviet Fiction since
Ivan Denisovich'. Zhores Medvedev, a geneticist, who like not a few
Russian intellectuals countenances no 'two cultures', entitles his own book
on Solzhenitsyn *10 Years after Ivan Denisovich*. Some knowledge of the
text was to percolate down to all strata, even where the reading of serious
fiction was not widespread. When Solzhenitsyn was arrested in 1974 and
spent the night in Lefortovo prison prior to his expulsion to the West, he
shared a cell with two small-time blackmarketeers; they asked why he had
been arrested and he started his long story by asking them if they had read
Ivan Denisovich. 'N-no. But we've heard about it. Are you Ivan Denisovich?'

was the response.[3] The work proved a stubborn benchmark: in *Literaturnaya gazeta* (*The Literary Gazette*) on 31 May 1995, in a front- page open letter to Solzhenitsyn, Olga Chaikovskaya appealed to the writer to speak out on the issue of the war in Chechnya, saying in part that thousands of innocent people were dying there, 'Ivan Denisovich and Matryona [the righteous heroine of Solzhenitsyn's story published by *Novy mir* in 1963. R.P.] are perishing over and over again'. In a thoroughly irreverent short story, first published in 1991, 'Solzhenitsyn, or a Voice from the Underground', very much in keeping with the new literary *mores* of the post-communist era, Igor Yarkevich (born in 1962, the year that *Ivan Denisovich* was published) writes:

> If I became Solly, I'd write lots of large-format works with heavyweight content, and in among these masterpieces there'd be *One Day in the Life of Ivan Denisovich* – the first swallow of the beginning of the approach of the anticipation of the end. Then I'd see quite different things from other people in the world around me, and I'd know how things stand – where the truth is, and where it isn't, and what to do so there would be truth, and how to carry on in general – but the way things are I'm just a miserable wanker who doesn't know a thing and got everything confused ages ago.[4]

To explain the immediate impact of *Ivan Denisovich* one needs to address the political and cultural climate of the time, and this is what will be done in this Introduction. Subsequent sections will examine the various aesthetic qualities of the novel, as perceived by the present critic and others, qualities which have ensured its universal and lasting value.

Nikita Khrushchev, Soviet leader from 1953 to 1964, was, it could be argued, the most important of all the dissidents before Gorbachev. In liberalising the system after Stalin's death, he created a climate in which dissenting intellectuals were able to express themselves more openly, some-times even in print. Yet Khrushchev himself was pointedly not of intellectual stock, and it became clear that he understood neither the aesthetic qualities of the artistic works he permitted (and/or sometimes castigated) nor the full political implications of his occasional acts of liberalisation in the sphere of the arts. It was not simply the case that events overtook him – as they frequently do Soviet/Russian leaders – but that a government, utterly convinced of its need to legislate for literature and the arts, yet suddenly embarked on a voyage into the liberalising unknown, was bound to be caught in contradiction. Khrushchev's policy zig-zags in the arts are well attested: Dudintsev's *Not by Bread Alone* was published, Pasternak's *Doctor Zhivago* was banned; the First Secretary's notorious outburst at an exhibition of avant-garde art at the Manezh Gallery on 1 December 1962 ('Are you a pederast? [...] We aren't going to spend a kopeck on this dog's shit.')[5] was counter-balanced by the publication of *Ivan Denisovich*.

There were, of course, specific political circumstances in each of these cases that could help to explain the given official attitude, but some of the incoherence in the policy towards the arts could be put down, at least in part, to two overriding factors: firstly, the very nature of the subject – Ronald Hingley has pointed out that 'the profession of letters has lent itself less to institutionalization than any other, except perhaps the oldest of all';[6] and secondly, the very curious relationship between the political leadership and the intelligentsia. There is no denying that intellectuals were relatively easy to tame, and many of them became victims of political persecution, but the Soviet leaders also held some intellectuals in awe. It has been suggested that Pasternak survived the great purges not least because Stalin viewed him almost as a *yurodivyi*, a God's fool, such was the writer's saint-like innocence, and, it must be said, his naivety. Vladimir Tendryakov completed in 1974 a work (published eventually in 1988) *On the Blessed Island of Communism* which offers a close-up of Khrushchev and his entourage. It concerns a meeting, typical of the time, and still very much a feature of Russian public life, between the political leaders and prominent members of the intelligentsia. Only lightly fictionalised, it registers the much-respected author's misgivings about all politicians (Churchill is chided for his 'obtuseness'), but Tendryakov reserves his real fire for Khrushchev's 'stupidity'. Moreover, Khrushchev – as if one needed reminding – was unpredictable, and the thinking of politicians generally is 'banal'.[7] The author recalled a previous occasion when Khrushchev had lambasted the writers at a meeting and had singled out Margarita Aliger (Stalin Prize-winner and much travelled literary functionary, hardly a dissident fire-brand) for particular criticism because of her involvement with the newly-launched liberal anthology *Literaturnaya Moskva* (*Literary Moscow*). The most memorable episode in the story is when the First Secretary initially does badly in a shooting contest, then makes a remarkable recovery, whereupon Mzhavanadze (the head of the Georgian Communist Party), having at first done well and been awarded a prize of a gilded statuette, swaps it with his boss, since his boss's statuette has less gilt on it. The vanity and pettiness on display here – the Russian word *poshlost'* springs to mind – could not be greater. Yet in his memoirs Khrushchev could write:

> You can't regulate the development of literature, art, and culture with a stick or by barking orders. You can't lay down a furrow and then harness all your artists to make sure they don't deviate from the straight and narrow. If you try to control your artists too tightly, there will be no clashing of opinions, conse-quently no criticism, and consequently no truth. There will be just a gloomy stereotype, boring and useless. Not only will this stereotype fail to encourage the people to benefit from their art; it will poison and kill their relationship to art.[8]

The episode Tendryakov witnessed occurred on 17 July 1960. How would such a leader react some fourteen months later when extracts from *Ivan Denisovich* were read aloud to him?

The story of how an unknown author, writing on a theme that hitherto had been complete anathema, came to be published in the most prominent of the Soviet Union's literary journals provides us with more insight into the interaction in the Soviet Union between politics and the arts than any amount of theorising and model-construction might. In practice, the publication of works had little to do with 'the censor' as such, and more to do with writers' self-censorship coupled with editorial circumspection and alertness. That Soviet censorship was based to a degree on a canon of prohibited topics there could be no doubt. Equally, there could be no doubt that the rules and regulations regarding sensitive topics were frequently by-passed – sometimes by a subtle editor, sometimes because to ban the work of an established, and perhaps even establishment, author might create more of a political backlash at home and abroad than to permit it (such had been the case with *Doctor Zhivago*, Khrushchev had admitted: 'I'm truly sorry for the way I behaved towards Pasternak [...] As a result we caused much harm to the Soviet Union. Because of the step we took, the intelligentsia abroad rose up against the Soviet Union, including those members of the intelligentsia who were not against socialism.')[9]; and sometimes – perhaps most frequently – because of a chance concatenation of artistic talent, political circumstances and personalities. Indeed, given the long length and stirring events of Solzhenitsyn's biography, his career as a published Soviet writer, lasting only from November 1962 to January 1966, would seem to smack of a fluke, of almost an aberration.

Briefly, in the case of *Ivan Denisovich* talent, politics and personalities came together as follows.

From his school and university days, through war service and during his time in prison, labour camp and exile in Central Asia, Solzhenitsyn had been an incorrigible and compulsive writer, composing in his head when captivity periodically denied him the possibility of committing things to paper. His return to society and legality gave him even more scope for creative activity. Between May and October 1959, while a teacher of mathematics in Ryazan, he returned to an idea which had occurred to him when he had been working as a convict brick-layer in the labour camp at Ekibastuz in 1950-1.[10] The plan was to describe the whole of labour camp existence in terms of just one single day, a day 'in the life of an average and in no way remarkable prisoner from morning till night'. Solzhenitsyn called his story provisionally *Shch-854*, that is, using the serial number which all prisoners were obliged to wear, to designate his hero, rather than giving him a name. Solzhenitsyn was 40 years old. He had served an inordinately long and – if one excepts some *juvenilia* which he came to discount – almost entirely underground literary apprenticeship, showing his works to only a few trusted and respected close acquaintances.

He had tried his hand at novels, plays, poetry, short stories and sketches. His qualities as a writer had been tested only by his own instincts and conscience and by the reactions of private individuals. He had never had to horse-trade with conformist editors over how his texts might have to be pruned or toned down to stand a chance of publication. He had not been corrupted by official flattery and literary prizes. He had never, as yet, had to heed the rebukes, be they condescending or caustic, of reviewers; he had never, as yet, been exposed to the righteous indignation of spot-welders and milkmaids, so outraged by what they had learnt of him that they were moved, in all probability at the instigation of those who had supplied them with the 'information', to write to the newspapers. Of course, Solzhenitsyn's values and ideas had been fashioned by his everyday experiences as a *zek* (convict), but perhaps of much more importance was that they had been cultivated and honed by *free* interaction with other individuals, often intellectuals, without any deference to officially sanctioned notions. This lack of intellectual inhibition is graphically illustrated in his novel *The First Circle* where the *sharashka* (special prison) inmates are considerably freer, and therefore more inquiring and boldly imaginative, than the writers and members of Stalin's élite, who persistently have to watch their words. The model for one of those inmates was to become one of the personalities instrumental in Solzhenitsyn's literary début.

The political context in which Solzhenitsyn felt that his story would stand a chance of publication has been examined at length by historians, social scientists and literary critics. Khrushchev's own motivation and achievements will continue to be debated, especially now that we have the added perspective of the Gorbachev era and its aftermath. Solzhenitsyn himself has argued in *The Gulag Archipelago* that even in the last year or so of Stalin's rule the labour camp system was staggering towards collapse, with escapes and mutinies becoming more frequent. In his account of the work stoppage and hunger strike which took place in Ekibastuz in January 1952 (exactly one year after that in which *Ivan Denisovich* is set) he tells us that 'The Special Camp system was beginning to collapse in one place after another, but our Father and Teacher [i.e. Stalin, R.P.] had no inkling of it – it was not, of course, reported to him [...] Evidently, the Stalinist camp system, particularly in the Special Camps, was nearing a crisis at the beginning of the fifties. Even in the Almighty One's lifetime the natives were beginning to tear at their chains.'[11] It has also been argued that the literary thaw of the mid-1950s in fact had its seeds in the last year of Stalin's rule, and that a totalitarian system did not automatically mean complete uniformity;[12] however, it is hard to see how there could have been any significant shift to 'pluralism', had Stalin lived longer, and particularly given the 'Doctors' Plot' of 1952. In any event, it is clear that Khrushchev's liberalisation policies did not appear entirely out of the blue.

Like all thinking men and women in the Soviet Union, Solzhenitsyn watched the political developments in Moscow, as they were revealed in the official media, with keen interest. One recalls the episode in *Cancer Ward* where Rusanov, the archetypal Stalinist, is shocked that in *Pravda* for 5 March 1955, the second anniversary of Stalin's death, the dictator is no longer mourned, when just two months previously, the date of his birthday had given rise to the usual gushing eulogies. By contrast, Kostoglotov, the ex-con and to some extent Solzhenitsyn's *porte-parole*, recalls the prisoners' rejoicing at the news of Stalin's death and how their reaction clashed with the public expressions of grief that he later learned had occurred.[13] Similarly, *Cancer Ward*, through the figure of Dyoma, reminds us of the importance of Vladimir Pomerantsev's article 'On Sincerity in Literature' in *Novy mir* of December 1953, which was very much a harbinger of the cultural thaw.[14] Dyoma's enthusiasm for Pomerantsev's view is challenged by Rusanov's daughter Avieta, the trainee literary hack, armed as she is with her recent experiences among Moscow's official intelligentsia.[15]

The Union of Soviet Writers held its Second Congress on 15-26 December 1954, 20 years after its First, despite the initial decision that they should be held much more frequently, possibly every three years, as envisaged in the Union's Constitution. (There had been intervening Congresses at Republic level.) The Union membership, standing at 3695, was now more than twice what it had been at its inauguration, its specific gravity in terms of Communist Party membership was a good deal higher – in 1934 of the 597 participating delegates 356 were Party members; in 1954 of the 720 participating dele- gates 522 were party members.[16] Moreover, the average age of the delegates had risen since the 1934 First Congress, a trend which was to continue with subsequent Congresses.[17] All these facts hardly suggested a liberal and reforming atmosphere. However, Stalin was dead, and some key liberal voices such as Kaverin and Erenburg were heard. Thus, Avieta reflects perfectly the turmoil that the average aspiring literary mediocrity might feel. The Third Congress of Soviet Writers, representing some 4,800 members, all – in theory at least – practising members of the Soviet intelligentsia, opened on 18 May 1959. On the very same day, an unknown schoolmaster in Ryazan set to work on a story about an uneducated peasant, who, in the eyes of those who had imprisoned him, did not even have a name.

This Third Congress came in the wake of monumental political develop- ments. In his 'secret speech' to the 20th Party Congress in February 1956, Khrushchev had openly attacked Stalin's 'cult of personality' and his 'intolerance, brutality and abuse of power'. Thousands upon thousands of political prisoners had been released, Solzhenitsyn among them. Having completed his prison sentence and living in administrative exile 'in perpe- tuity' in Kok Terek in Kazakhstan, he had received a letter from the regional MVD (Ministry of Internal Affairs) in April 1956 informing him that his sentence was annulled and his term of exile was at an end.[18] The shockwaves that were sent throughout the communist world by the secret speech led to rebellions in Poland and Hungary, as some sections of the body politic in these Soviet satellites felt that total independence from Moscow was now a possibility. Though they were rudely disabused of this – in the case of Hungary with Soviet tanks – it was clear to some in the Kremlin that Khrushchev's de-Stalinisation policies were explosive and could lead to the break-up of the Soviet empire.

Consequently, in June 1957 Malenkov, Molotov and Kaganovich headed a faction within the Praesidium which outvoted the First Secretary. Khrushchev out-manoeuvred what he dubbed this 'anti-Party group' by appealing to the full membership of the Party's Central Committee, consigning the leaders of the opposition to the political wilderness. It was perhaps a sign of the healthier times that the wilderness his opponents now found themselves in was considerably more comfortable and metaphorical than the one that Solzhenitsyn had had to endure. In October Khrushchev dismissed Marshal Zhukov from his post as Minister of Defence, and in March 1958 assumed the premiership of the Soviet Union himself. His de-Stalinisation policies seemed secure. Some sections of the intelligentsia now had every reason to feel optimistic; and such must have been the feelings of many liberal writers as the Third Congress of Soviet Writers appoached. However, this turned out to be something of a lack-lustre affair, with routine speeches and quasi-conservative pronouncements to counter-balance the liberal voices.

What had happened to emasculate this set-piece of literary life was literature itself, for 1958 had seen the rejection of *Doctor Zhivago* for publication in the Soviet Union and subsequently Pasternak's having to decline the Nobel Prize. Already with an outstanding literary reputation at home and abroad, Pasternak found himself at the centre of an international scandal. Pasternak was expelled from the Writers' Union and even found himself forced to write to the First Secretary begging to be allowed to remain in Russia. Here was a chill warning to the writers.

On the other hand there were the writers themselves – and more precisely a new and unruly wave of poets and prose writers who were too young to have suffered at first hand themselves in the 1930s purges, but who had relatives who had suffered, and these writers were galvanised by the new freedom, albeit partial and unpredictable, that the post-Stalin era afforded. By the late 1950s Evtushenko, Akhmadulina, Voznesensky, Okudzhava and Aksyonov were about to burst on the scene. They were inspired by the untainted example of Pasternak, and they were no doubt excited by cultural developments in the West involving rock-and-roll and 'angry young men'. The literary world was beginning to polarise between Stalinist conservatives and liberals, the former associated with the journal *Oktyabr'*, edited by Vsevolod Kochetov, and the latter forming around Alexander Tvardovsky's *Novy mir*.

In October 1961 the Communist Party of the Soviet Union held its 22nd Congress, and this saw a renewed emphasis on de-Stalinisation. Tvardovsky was editor of *Novy mir* from 1950 to 1954 and again from 1958 to 1970. In addition, he was for many years a top-ranking bureaucrat, notably as Secretary of the Board of the Writers' Union of the Soviet Union 1950-54 and again 1959-71. He was also a deputy of the Supreme Soviet, and under Khrushchev became a member of the Party's Central Committee. The most startling political gesture to come out of the 22nd Party Congress was the removal of Stalin's body from the Mausoleum, where it had lain next to Lenin's. The most engrossing things that were said at the Congress, as far as the writers were concerned, included Tvardovsky's contribution. It called on writers to take full advantage of the opportunities opened up by the 20th Party Congress and to depict the 'labour' and 'ordeals' of the people.

Solzhenitsyn was excited and at the same time torn by all these signals. On the one hand they were an invitation to submit for publication any number of the works he had written for the desk drawer. On the other hand, there was every reason to be afraid that he could again find himself charged with anti-Soviet activity. When he was a captain in the Red Army and had been twice decorated, private correspondence to a friend, Nikolai Vitkevich, had cost Solzhenitsyn 11 years of prison and exile; how much more incriminating could be the deepest thoughts and harsh experiences of an ex-con who had found the time, energy and skill to set them out on paper in carefully wrought sentences and at great length? The Party line could change so quickly – it very nearly had in 1957 when the 'anti-Party group' had mounted its offensive; and indeed it did change in October 1964 when Khrushchev was forcibly retired. There must have been another major consideration in Solzhenitsyn's mind: if he, and the other brave, honest and intelligent spirits that he had encountered over the years, spoke out, surely that would help pave the way to reform. No less than in the days of Pushkin and Dostoevsky, literature and politics, at least in the context of Russia, were inextricably linked. A character in *The First Circle* was to put the notion most succinctly, in words that have become much quoted: 'Having a great writer is like having a second government'.[19] Would Solzhenitsyn, a fighter by nature and with a pronounced sense of justice, ever again have such an opportunity? But the misgivings stayed with him right up until the day he agreed to have his story submitted: 'How could I, without any duress, have turned in a denunciation of myself?'[20]

The author may well have been remote from public life, but he was not isolated. Some of his trusted acquaintances had read and admired his work, and some of them were better connected than he was. Solzhenitsyn first met Lev Kopelev in the *sharashka* as described in *The First Circle* – he appears as Lev Rubin. By the time they met, Solzhenitsyn's faith in Marxism had been severely dented, but Kopelev was still utterly convinced of the validity of Marx's doctrine and indeed of Stalin's infallibility. Kopelev was rehabilitated in 1956 and had his Party membership restored the following year. In the late 1950s, then, his ideological orientation allowed him, more easily than some, to return to the mainstream of intellectual life in Russia after his rehabilitation, while his intelligence and sincerity kept him for many years in Solzhenitsyn's affections. True, the two men were to have serious intellectual differences over the years, and it should be noted that after being expelled from the Party again, in 1968, Kopelev was led to revise radically his attitude to Marxism.

Kopelev was, and still is, a specialist in Polish and German literature and culture, best known in his day in the former Soviet Union for his translations of German literature and for works on Goethe and Brecht, which were published in the 1960s. He was also a friend of Heinrich Böll. From the early 1970s he started to publish works in the West which were unacceptable at home, notably his volumes of memoirs. He emigrated to West Germany in 1980. Until 1968 he was employed by the Moscow Institute of Art History. In addition to their conflicting ideological positions, Solzhenitsyn and Kopelev had other differences. Kopelev, born in March 1912, was more than six years older than Solzhenitsyn. He had been a junior university lecturer in the Moscow Institute of Philosophy, Literature and History, before the war, just at the time when Solzhenitsyn, resident in Rostov-on-Don, had been taking his correspondence course in literature from there. Kopelev was a flamboyant and outward-going character. His Marxist outlook notwithstanding, he displayed an irreverent sense of humour, which, one suspects, was conditioned not least by his knowledge of world literature: one chapter of a book that he wrote together with his second wife Raisa Orlova covering the years 1956-80 (*We Lived in Moscow*) is entitled 'Moderate Progress within the Boundaries of the Law' in clear reference to the delightfully anarchistic book by the Czech writer, Jaroslav Hašek. Kopelev was also, apparently, the chief architect of the wickedly satirical version of *The Lay of Igor* which the prisoners in *The First Circle* stage. Generally, Solzhenitsyn's writing is not characterised by the sort of comedy that might raise a laugh. Come the late 1950s and early 60s, Kopelev was in the thick of Moscow literary life, well-informed and well-connected at home and abroad. The prominent American journalist Robert Kaiser, writing in 1976, informs us that in the Kopelevs' flat the telephone hardly ever stopped ringing and that there was a steady stream of friends, relatives and neighbours dropping in.[21] By contrast, Solzhenitsyn was a man who jealously tried to guard his privacy, to the point of becoming, in the eyes of many, a recluse. In his last years in the Soviet Union, and also in his time in emigration, meetings with the writer were restricted, being arranged, even with a degree of stage management, by intermediaries.

When, in June 1956, Solzhenitsyn returned from Central Asian exile to Moscow, resolved to find work in the Russian provinces, he was met at the station by Kopelev and Panin (the other of the author's closest friends from the *sharashka*, and the one who had accompanied him in 1950 to the special regime camp in Ekibastuz. He appears as Sologdin in *The First Circle*). Through visits and correspondence the friendship remained firm. Some months before the 22nd Party Congress, Solzhenitsyn had lodged a copy of what was to become known as *One Day in the Life of Ivan Denisovich* with Kopelev, and they had even drawn up a list of writers to whom it might be shown.[22] Curiously, Kopelev was by no means as enthusiastic about the work as had been several of the others entrusted to read it. He dismissed it as 'a typical production story in the spirit of Socialist Realism'.[23] Be that as it may, he and his wife were resolved to do all they could to see it published.

One of the lesser known aspects of literary life in Soviet Russia concerned the role of women – not as outstanding poets, playwrights, fiction writers and memoirists, of whom there are many shining examples – but in the less glamorous fields of copy-editing, negotiating between chief editors and authors, mediating, and what in the Western world of publishing and the media is often called 'facilitating'. Of course, the really mundane business of typing and filing often fell to women; but there was also the all-important work of *preserving*, of creating archives. Modern Russian literature owes a lot to wives and widows in this respect. On the surface, the Soviet publishing world, like the political élite in general, was very much a man's domain: men held nearly all the positions of responsibility in the Writers' Union, in the mainstream literary journals and in the publishing houses. The glaring exception to this was the figure of Ekaterina Furtseva, Minister of Culture from 1960 to 1974 and butt of many a dissident joke regarding her aesthetic sensibilities; and no doubt she had numerous clones throughout the system, as epitomised by Avieta Rusanova in *Cancer Ward*. But just below the surface of this man's world stood a formidable army of highly educated, aesthetically sophisticated and committed females. Solzhenitsyn's first and second wives (both Natalya) have played major roles in his career, not least as *confidantes*. Other women played a more purely professional role.

At the time of the 22nd Party Congress, Kopelev's relations with the staff at *Novy mir* were hardly good. He was involved in the production of a liberal anthology called *Tarusa Pages* and this had led, paradoxically, to clashes with Tvardovsky and others. Therefore, it was felt more politic that Kopelev's wife should deliver Solzhenitsyn's manuscript. Moreover, it was important that the right person on the editorial staff should be approached, and in the right manner.

In the second week of November 1961, Raisa Orlova handed in the story *Shch-854* to Anna Berzer, who worked in the prose section of *Novy mir*, with strict instructions that the manuscript should be passed straight to Tvardovsky. Easier said than done, for there were several rungs between Berzer and the Editor-in-Chief of the most prominent literary journal in the Soviet Union. Tvardovsky might simply set aside this work by an unknown author, or more likely, pass it down to one of his minions, for a reader's report or 'internal review' as it is called in Russia, and the outcome could be unpredictable. Berzer's immediate boss, whom by rights she ought to have approached in the first instance, was the circumspect Evgeny Gerasimov. Berzer had the manuscript retyped in a more readable format and got Kopelev to provide it with an author. His sense of fun did not desert him: *Shch-584* was to be the work of one 'A. Ryazansky', echoing Solzhenitsyn's place of residence. She then applied a little psychology to get Tvardovsky to read it himself 'cold', so to speak: she asked several of her immediate superiors, quite baldly, if they were interested in looking at a story about 'the camps' and they all demurred. She now had a clear field. She took Solzhenitsyn's story and Lidiya Chukovskaya's *Sofia Petrovna* (likewise a work to do with the purges, but relating to the 1930s and the intelligentsia) straight to the top, and asked which one the Editor-in-Chief would like to read first, pointing out that the former was about 'a prison camp, seen through the eyes of a peasant'.[24] The work was by a complete unknown, whereas Chukovskaya, of course, had an established literary pedigree.

It was a quirk of literary life that Tvardovsky, an accomplished poet, as it turned out, was not himself a particularly good judge of poetry, and his journal will always be remembered mainly for the prose that it dared to publish in the late 1950s and 60s. Tvardovsky was of peasant stock, enormously popular during the war years for his morale-boosting narrative poem about a simple Soviet soldier *Vasily Tyorkin*. He was also in the dissident camp, most notably for *Tyorkin in the Other World*, a parody depicting hell as the Soviet state, which did just squeeze into print before Khrushchev's fall from power, and for his poem *By Right of Memory* (written in the late 1960s). This work was published abroad, and in part redressed the rosy picture of collectivisation Tvardovsky had painted in his *Land of Muravia* of 1936; the later poem disclosed how his own father had been a victim of dekulakisation. Tvardovsky was firmly of the opinion that the Soviet system was capable of reform and that literature could play a vital role in the process. Under his tutelage *Novy mir* became the flagship of liberalisation, and many felt that his removal as its editor in 1970 hastened his death the following year. Solzhenitsyn's relations with Tvardovsky were to be by no means untroubled. One anecdote might suffice to illustrate some of the qualities of the man that both attracted and repelled Solzhenitsyn: in May 1964 when Tvardovsky visited Solzhenitsyn in Ryazan and read the manuscript of *The First Circle*, he consumed vast quantities of cognac and vodka, according to the author, and told him: 'You're a terrible person. If I came to power, I'd *put you in prison*'.[25] By and large, Solzhenitsyn was not the sort of man to approve of either Tvardovsky's well-attested, immoderate drinking, or of his sense of irony. Be that as it may, Berzer's machinations brought about, at the outset, an extraordinary meeting of minds and sensibilities. It was 7 December 1961.

As was his habit, Tvardovsky took the manuscript home to read in bed, which he started to do the next evening, 8 December. The story goes that, having started on the work, he got out of bed, got dressed and read throughout the night.

By morning he was bursting with excitement.[26] He contacted several close colleagues including Kopelev, and was delighted to learn that 'A. Ryazansky' was a genuine new writer, and not someone he already knew indulging in a bit of mystification. A telegram was promptly despatched to Solzhenitsyn inviting him to Moscow, and the following Tuesday, 12 December, the day after his forty-third birthday found him, escorted by Kopelev, in the editorial offices of *Novy mir*. The meeting went splendidly, and Solzhenitsyn readily agreed to one key change in his text, for none of the editorial board liked its working title – they settled instead on *Odin den' Ivana Denisovicha* (literally: 'Ivan Denisovich's One Day'). The author was given a contract and a handsome advance. That the work deserved publication there could be no doubt, but Tvardovsky was going to have to perform some very adept footwork to achieve this. He was closely connected with many leading public figures, including Khrushchev himself, but there were still a great many Stalinists in office (as Evtushenko's poem *The Heirs of Stalin* of 1962 was to remind everyone). Simply to have the story set in type and then submitted to the censorship could easily result in rejection, emasculation, delay or even denunciation to the security forces. The last possible outcome had, in fact, been the case with Vasily Grossman's *Life and Fate*, which was submitted to *Znamya* in October 1960 and in February 1961 was 'arrested'. The Party's chief ideologist Mikhail Suslov later, in July 1962, summoned Grossman, and in a meeting that lasted for three hours, likened his book to an atom bomb, and said it would not be published for another 250-300 years.[27] (In fact, *Life and Fate* was eventually published in the Soviet Union in 1988.)

Moreover, there were political differences between the various members of Tvardovsky's team. Solzhenitsyn was very impressed by Berzer, but his memoirs are less than flattering to some others, perhaps not as brave, perhaps not as well-placed as the editor-in-chief... Tvardovsky started by showing Solzhenitsyn's text to prominent writers whom he trusted and several of these wrote highly favourable reports on it – these could be used in any future tussle with the authorities over the work. Though Tvardovsky tried to limit the circulation of the work, his security could not be foolproof, and quickly Solzhenitsyn became, as the saying went in the Soviet literary world, 'widely known in small circles'. Thanks to Tvardovsky – but no doubt to others too, possibly Kopelev – some of Russia's leading authors immediately became Solzhenitsyn fans, notably Samuil Marshak and Kornei Chukovsky (whose daughter's novel had been presented to Tvardovsky on 7 December 1961 as a rival for his attention). Within a matter of weeks the story of Stalin's labour camps was common knowledge to an ever-widening circle of Moscow's *intelligenty*.

Tvardovsky, Dementyev, one of *Novy mir*'s two deputy editors (Gerasimov was the other) and Lakshin (a 'new boy', in that he was only confirmed as a member of the editorial board in May 1962, but soon to become the journal's chief literary critic) drafted a letter to Khrushchev explaining that it was the unanimous opinion of the board that the work should be published, and quoting from some of the favourable internal reports they had collected on it. Tvardovsky passed the manuscript to Khrushchev's private secretary Vladimir Lebedev, who read the work and was in favour of it – subject to some changes. All this took some time, which must have seemed all the more irksome to Solzhenitsyn, especially given the flurry of activity that had taken place when Tvardovsky first read the work. Be that as it may, Solzhenitsyn was summoned to an editorial meeting at *Novy mir* on 23 July 1962, which the author later recalled as being 'difficult'.[28] Some of the criticism and suggestions voiced at this meeting are discussed in the next chapter.

Solzhenitsyn agreed to work on the text some more, and may well have been helped in this by Anna Berzer. She also arranged for him to socialise with some of the capital's other writers – they were anxious to meet this new voice. Berzer's office was often the scene of informal get-togethers, and on the evening of 26 July Solzhenitsyn met Vladimir Voinovich, Viktor Nekrasov and Naum Korzhavin among others.

In early August Tvardovsky sent the revised manuscript to Lebedev along with the letter that had been drafted to Khrushchev and a selection of favourable reports. Khrushchev was spending the summer in the Crimea. The American poet Robert Frost visited him there, accompanied by Aleksei Surkov and Lebedev. The American and Soviet poets apparently discussed *Ivan Denisovich* in the leader's presence. Khrushchev insisted on seeing the work – Lebedev apparently read extracts to him some time between the 9 and 14 September. According to Lakshin, on the 15 or 16 September Lebedev telephoned Tvardovsky at home with the news that Khrushchev liked the work.[29] Yet there was no official statement. Apparently also, Khrushchev and Mikoyan said that they both approved of the story and it should be published. But what happened next almost beggared belief. There was a five-day silence, with Solzhenitsyn, Tvardovsky and no doubt a good many others waiting with bated breath, before Tvardovsky received a message from the Central Committee on 21 September, ordering him to provide twenty-three copies of the text – by the next day. The episode is strongly reminiscent of Stalin's injunction to the Moscow Art Theatre to resurrect Bulgakov's play *The Days of the Turbins* for the dictator's personal consideration. Solzhenitsyn's biographer Michael Scammell describes graphically what happened next:

> Tvardovsky was flabbergasted. He did not possess twenty-three copies. He had deliberately kept the number down so as not to let the story circulate (he was unaware of just how many *were* circulating, and it was certainly not his fault). To type up twenty-three copies was out of the question in a single night, so he grasped at the only other possibility: a limited printing of the necessary copies. *Novy Mir* didn't have its

own presses, it was a dependency of *Izvestia.* Tvardovsky
rang the head of *Izvestia*'s printing department and arranged
to have four machines set aside from printing *Izvestia* that
night and reserved for printing twenty-five copies of *Ivan
Denisovich.*

Berzer and Kondratovich [Tvardovsky's second deputy
editor, after Dementyev. R.P.] were put in charge of the
operation and allotted four proof-readers and an equivalent
number of type-setters. For the latter the text presented major
problems of style, spelling, and vocabulary. It was a far cry
from the dull and cliché-ridden speeches of government
leaders. Nor did the unorthodox nature of the contents escape
them, though they were sworn to secrecy about this strange
project. They worked feverishly through the night, and
at dawn the next morning the copies were bound in the
distinctive light-blue covers of *Novy Mir* and the plates
locked away in the *Izvestia* strong-room. Later that morning
twenty-three copies were delivered to the offices of the
Central Committee and the remaining two to Tvardovsky
(one of which he later presented to Solzhenitsyn).[30]

This account also, of course, reminds us of publishing and printing
procedures before the days of desk-top techniques, computers, and even,
especially in the case of the Soviet Union in the very early 1960s, the general
availability and quality of photocopying.

After this second burst of activity, Solzhenitsyn's story was then distrib-
uted to the members of the Praesidium and was discussed at some length in
a meeting or meetings. Then Tvardovsky was informed, at first by Lebedev
informally on 15 October, and then when he was summoned for a meeting
with the First Secretary himself a few days later, that the work could be
published. Lebedev tried to persuade the author to make one more change
in the text, wanting Tyurin's remark – to the effect that God does exist after
all and when He strikes He strikes hard – to be removed. After some reflection,
Solzhenitsyn felt that he could make no more concessions. The matter was
not taken any further and *One Day in the Life of Ivan Denisovich* appeared
in the November issue of *Novy mir.* The storm broke.

The path from obscurity to publication and fame, from Solzhenitsyn, to
Kopelev, to Berzer, to Tvardovsky, to Lebedev and then to Khrushchev was
by no means straightforward. There were potential pot-holes and diversions
along the way. It is true that Solzhenitsyn was lucky. It is equally true that
his work was allowed publication because a volatile political leader, beset
with problems over his economic policies and the Cuba crisis, both of which
led to his humiliation, was desperate for a solution, and must have thought,
in part, that he could save himself by a poignant reminder to all those who

mattered of the 'bad old days' under Stalin. But the degree of serendipity was surely outweighed by the intrinsic qualities of the text itself. All those who came into contact with it were shaken and moved – some were frightened by it, but many more were stirred to champion it.

I. Russian Texts and English Translations

The obvious reason for comparing various earlier drafts of a given work is to discover how the writer's mind was operating as he re-worked, discarded, added and substituted. Thus one gains a fuller appreciation of the finished article. However, in the case of Soviet literature there is an added element – namely the ideological requirements that the author may feel obliged to meet if he wants his work published. Should the demands of the author's conscience and the party line coincide then the writer has no problem. And indeed there have been numerous cases of Soviet works being re-written willingly in order to toe the Party line. Gladkov's *Cement* went through more than 20 redactions, with major new editions after its initial appearance in 1925 – in 1932, 1947, 1950 and 1958.[1] Leonov's *The Thief* and Sholokhov's *The Quiet Don* underwent major re-workings for publication and/or republication, in the case of the latter one suspects very much with the strictures of Socialist Realism in mind. Solzhenitsyn became involved in the controversy over this work's authorship when he prefaced a short book, anonymously written and brought out by an émigré publisher, which sought uncompromisingly to dismiss Sholokhov as the author. Solzhenitsyn cited the judgement of Solomon: would the real author, like the real mother of a child, allow his progeny to be cut in half?[2]

There are also practical considerations: a new author will almost certainly have to take advice from his editor, whereas a more established writer will have more bargaining power. In the Soviet context both editor and writer realised that they would have to get the work past *Glavlit*, the censorship. In the case of *Ivan Denisovich*, Solzhenitsyn made a few small concessions in his dealings with *Novy mir*, but to a very large extent the work was as the author wished it to be.

After his expulsion to the West, Solzhenitsyn stated that with the exception of *The Gulag Archipelago* all his works had been toned down in the hope that they would one day be published legally in the Soviet Union. There must have been concern among many critics that Solzhenitsyn, now free to write as he pleased but divorced from his target audience, might re-work his texts to shake the West out of its bourgeois complacency and thus make them less artistic and more tendentious. (After all, that was roughly what had happened to those Soviet works in the 1920s and 30s which underwent

changes in the light of their authors' 'developing' political perceptions...).
In some instances, Solzhenitsyn was now, indeed, accused of re-working
his texts rather than restoring them.

Yet by and large this did not happen. The one work that saw the biggest
changes was *August 1914*, the first volume of the historical cycle *The Red
Wheel*, and anyway, this could be regarded as 'work in progress'. In any
event it was necessary for Solzhenitsyn to put his literary house in order,
for he had had little control over the way his works were circulating in the
West: there were several versions of *Cancer Ward* and especially *The First
Circle*. The author had even less control over the translations of his works
(with Western publishers' commercial interests sometimes taking prece-
dence over their devotion to literature – the first English translation of
August 1914 in particular had been spoilt by undue haste), let alone the
sometimes ludicrous travesties which were perpetrated when some of his
works were transferred to screen or stage. Honourable exceptions to this
would include the film of *Ivan Denisovich* starring Tom Courtenay and
Clifford Williams' production of the play *The Love-Girl and the Innocent*.

In discussing the various versions of the text one can do worse than to
start with the note to the Vermont-Paris 1973 edition, the authorised one:

> *One Day in the Life of Ivan Denisovich* – conceived by the
> author when he was employed on general work in the
> Ekibastuz Special camp in the winter of 1950-51. It was
> produced in 1959, first of all as 'Shch – 854 (One Day of
> One Con', politically sharper. It was softened in 1961 – and
> made suitable in that form for submission to *Novy mir*
> in the autumn of that year. Furthermore, as a concession to
> the requirements for it to be printed, the figure of the captain
> of Second Rank was freed from any humorous traits and
> a single reference to Stalin, which hadn't been there
> before, was introduced. The decision to print the story was
> taken by the Politbureau of the Central Committee of the
> Communist Party of the Soviet Union in October 1962
> under Khrushchev's personal pressure. It was printed in
> *Novy mir*, 1962, no.11, and then by the *Soviet Writer*
> publishing house (100 thousand copies), and in paperback
> [*roman-gazeta*] (700 thousand) in 1971-72. All these edi-
> tions were destroyed in the libraries on secret instructions.
> The first completely undistorted edition was produced by
> the YMCA-Press publishing house in Paris, 1973.
>
> The character of *Ivan Denisovich* was formed from private
> Shukhov, who fought alongside the author in the Soviet-German
> war (and was never in prison), from general experience of
> prisoners and the personal experience of the author while

working as a brick-layer in the Special camp. The other
figures are all from camp life with their original biographies.

The three Soviet texts which Solzhenitsyn mentions here are all very close,
though there are minor variations. The authorised version differs significantly from these, but is not entirely the pre-softened text that the author
originally produced, without an eye to publication. Solzhenitsyn has given
us his own account in *The Calf Butted the Oak* of the changes that he made
during his dealings with the editorial staff of *Novy mir*. One scholar has
made a close study of the whole matter and the various texts, and writes:

> To sum up the Paris edition, we may say that it is a final text
> incorporating elements from all stages in its history. Rather
> than consider it an anomaly, we may look on it as a text
> which benefitted from the constraint of its author, as might
> any text, but also from the contraint of others involved in its
> first publication, which again is not so uncommon. A restric-
> tive environment may stimulate creative discoveries in an
> author, and the act of censorship itself may contain 'creative
> moments'. The Paris edition, while essentially restorative,
> takes advantage of such moments and fixes them as final by
> the free decision of the author. The Soviet editions are not
> thereby abolished, but rather converted into historical docu-
> ments, necessary for an understanding of the literature of the
> time and the development of the individual text.[3]

The most self-evident suggestion from the *Novy mir* board, which Solzhenitsyn
accepted and never went back on, concerns the title of the work. Here one
might detect a purely practical consideration. *Ivan Denisovich* had become
so famous under the *Novy mir* title that to revert to *Shch-854* after all these
years might simply confuse an already admiring readership.

Solzhenitsyn did undoubtedly make concessions, which in the Paris edition
he was able to go back on. However, the process was very much one of
negotiation. The author was able to comply with some of the requests that came
from Khrushchev's private secretary, Lebedev, particularly regarding the figure
of Captain Buynovsky (see below), and the liberal use of the derogatory term
gad, especially as directed at the camp guards. However, he was unable, as
Lebedev wanted, to give the prisoners any hope of release. One request which
was ironic in the extreme, given the circumstances, the author was able to meet.
Lebedev wanted some mention of Stalin, of which – quite deliberately so on
the author's part – there was none in the original text. This was an engaging
instance of the anti-Stalinists out-Heroding Herod.

Tvardovsky's first deputy editor, Alexander Dementyev, the most
reactionary of individuals on the *Novy mir* staff, according to Solzhenitsyn,
wanted many more changes, including the deletion of the conversation

between the Captain and Tsezar about the film *The Battleship Potyomkin*, the deletion of the conversation between Ivan and Alyoshka about God, and that the references to the *Benderovtsy* (followers of Bendera, the Ukrainian nationalist) be re-worked to depict them in an ideologically correct fashion as murderers of the Soviet people. The author responded: 'I've waited ten years already, and I can wait another ten years. I'm in no hurry. My life doesn't depend on literature. Give me my manuscript back, and I'll go away.'[4] Tvardovsky immediately intervened to tell Solzhenitsyn he didn't *have* to do anything, but that everyone was anxious that the manuscript should 'get through'. At the eleventh hour (the first week in November 1962, when Solzhenitsyn was correcting the page proofs, Lebedev made one last request: that Tyurin's words to the effect that the Creator exists after all and when He strikes He strikes hard be removed (as noted in the previous chapter). The author, after reflection, was unable to comply, and the matter was never pursued.[5]

Gary Kern concludes his discussion of the various texts as follows:

> In sum, the canonical text restores many, but not necessarily all, of the passages deleted from the original manuscript *Šč-854*. It also retains some of the changes incorporated in the *Novy mir* text of *Odin den' Ivana Denisoviča*. The result is a text which is clearer, politically sharper and slightly less subtle, but more comprehensible and more religiously colored.[6]

Of the 52 instances, which Kern detects, where the authorised text and the *Novy mir* text differ, the following are perhaps the most instructive:

> 1. When Ivan is told to wash the floor as a punishment his ambivalent thoughts on the nature of work are reported as follows: (Paris text p. 14) Работа – она как палка, конца в ней два: для людей делаешь – качество дай, для начальника делаешь – дай показуху. The *Novy mir* text (p. 13) has дурака for начальника.

> 2. Immediately afterwards, when Ivan is having his breakfast, we are given a scene of the dining hall with a snapshot of one prisoner, the Benderite, in particular: (Paris text p.15) Там, за столом, ещё ложку не окунувши, парень молодой крестится. Бендеровец, значит, и то новичок: старые бендеровцы, в лагере пожив, от креста отстали. The *Novy mir* text (p.13) reads: Там, за столом, ещё ложку не окунумши, парень молодой крестится. Значит, украинец западный, и то новичок.

> 3. Before leaving the hut to go out and work, Ivan hears the baptist Alyoshka in the bunk above him reading the Gospels: (Paris text p.22) Баптист читал евангелие не вовсе про себя, а

как бы в дыхание (может. для Шухова нарочно. они ведь. эти баптисты, любят агитировать, вроде политруков). The *Novy mir* text (p. 17) omits the last two words here.

4. When the hero recalls the letters that his wife is allowed to send him twice a year, the difficulties on the collective farm are dwelt on, but the Paris edition paints a slightly fuller and harsher picture: the Paris text (p. 31) has: Колхоз укруп-нили — так его и ране укрупняли, а потом мельчили опять. Ну. ещё кто нормы трудодней не выполняет — огороды поджали до пятнадцати соток, а кому и под самый дом обрезали. Ещё, писала когда-то баба, был закон за норму ту судить и кто не выполнит — в тюрьму сажать, но как-то тот закон не вступил. The *Novy mir* text (p. 23) omits this last sentence.

5. When the column reaches the perimeter of the building site Alyoshka is pleased to see the sun coming up, and we learn that for the baptists the harshness of camp life is like water off a duck's back: the Paris text (pp. 33-34) has: По воскресеньям всё с другими баптистами шепчется. С них лагеря как с гуся вода. По двадцать пять лет вкатили им за баптистскую веру — неуж думают тем от веры отвадить? The *Novy mir* text (p. 24) omits this last sentence.

6. When the brick-laying is in full swing and Captain Buynovsky complains to his team leader about having to work with the workshy Fetyukov, the expletive he uses is toned down in the *Novy mir* text. The Paris text (p. 69) has: Поставь меня с человеком! Не буду я с этим м...ком носить! The *Novy mir* text (p. 44) has г...ком. The two ellipses stand for мудак (prick, fucker) and говнюк (shit).

7. When Captain Buynovsky explains how he knows so much about life on board the English fleet there is a major re-jigging of the text, with the authorised version incorporating mental and verbal interjections from the Captain's audience. The Paris text (pp. 84-85) has:

— А откуда вы так хорошо знаете быт английского флота? — спрашивают в соседней пятёрке.

— Да, видите ли, я прожил почти целый месяц на английском крейсере, имел там свою каюту. Я сопровождал морской конвой. Был офицером связи у них.

— Ах, вот как! Ну, уже достаточно, чтобы вмазать вам двадцать пять.

—Нет, знаете, этого либерального критицизма я не придерживаюсь.

Я лучшего мнения о нашем законодательстве.

(Дуди-дуди. Шухов про себя думает, не встревая. Сенька Клевшин с американцами два дня жил, так ему четвертную закатали, а ты месяц на ихем корабле околачивался, – так сколько ж тебе давать?)

– Но уже после войны английский адмирал, чёрт его дёрнул, прислал мне памятный подарок. "В знак благодарности". Удивляюсь и проклинаю!...

The *Novy mir* text (p. 53) has:

– А откуда вы так хорошо знаете быт английского флота? спрашивают в соседней пятёрке.

– Да. видите ли, я прожил почти месяв на английском крейсере, имел там свою каюту. Я сопровождал морской конвой. Был офицером связи у них. И ещё, представляете, после войны английский адмирал, чёрт его дёрнул, прислал мне памятный подарок. "В знак благодарности". Удивляюсь и проклинаю! .. И вот всех в кучу одну. с бендеровцами тут сидеть – удовольствие маленькое.

8. At supper Ivan notices in particular the old prisoner Yu-81. The Paris text (p. 102) has: Об этом старике говорили Шухову, что он по лагерям да по тюрьмам сидит несчётно, сколько советская власть стоит. и ни одна амнистия его не прикоснулась, а как одна десятка кончалась, так ему сразу новую совали. The *Novy mir* text (p. 64) omits the phrase сколько советская власть стоит.

Another general change between the two texts involves the word for God (*Bog*) (also Lord and Creator, *Gospodi* and *Sozdatel'*) being spelled with a lower case initial letter in the *Novy mir* text, in accordance with Soviet convention. (Indeed, in his Afterword to the first publication [in Paris] of *August 1914*, Solzhenitsyn wryly suggested that the reason the book was banned in the Soviet Union was because he refused to spell God with a small letter.) Capitals are restored in the authorised version of *Ivan Denisovich*.

To a large extent the eight examples of textual differences cited above speak for themselves, but two points require more comment. The last cited example shows the authorised version making a neat alliterative juxtaposition between *sidit* (be inside, in prison) and *stoit* (stands) – the assonance thus created (which no translation can adequately reproduce) equates the Soviet system with imprisonment. The major change, concerning Buynovsky (example 7), needs some explanation. Originally this character was conceived as a figure of fun at least in the eyes of Ivan Denisovich (through whom most of the reader's information is channelled), for Buynovsky is a former naval officer, a man used to exuding authority and inspiring respect; he has yet to learn the dog-eat-dog values that obtain in the camp and which the street-wise and resourceful Ivan, a man without education or social polish, understands far better. Lebedev wanted the satirical aspect of the Captain removed, no doubt so that he could be passed off more easily by established Soviet literary critics as a positive hero. We can see that Solzhenitsyn felt able to do this for the *Novy mir* edition, and likewise was able to attribute to Buynovsky, as requested, the 'correct', i.e. Soviet, evaluation of Bendera's followers (Bendera was a Ukrainian nationalist underground fighter). The authorised text restores some of Ivan's amused condescension at the Captain's naivety. It also leaves more open the question of the Ukrainian nationalists' collaboration with the Germans, by omitting Buynovsky's (negative) reference to them. Instead, we are left to rely on the narrator's rather bland allusion to one of 'Bendera's followers', whom he sees at breakfast crossing himself – a somewhat sympathy-inspiring detail, given the context. Moreover, the authorised version underlines the uncertainty factor in the characters' make-up: in a work that has been so rightly viewed as a polemic, one should not overlook the manner in which Solzhenitsyn is adept at showing differing perceptions of the same situation.

One final point about Buynovsky. In the *The Calf Butted the Oak*[7] Solzhenitsyn tells us that when in 1961, not knowing why, he revised his text and 'lightened' it, he omitted a 'long story' that the Captain tells Tsezar about the Americans being duped at Sevastopol in 1945 by 'our fictitious well-being' (*nashim podstavnym blagopoluchiem*). This passage is a good example of Solzhenitsyn's talent for exposing Soviet *pokazukha* or *tukhta* ('window-dressing'). The *Novy mir* text (p.68) has Buynovsky stating his delight at the bread baton Tsezar has received in his food parcel and about to recall an incident in Archangel – just before the guard comes to take him to the punishment cell. The authorised Paris edition (p.109) has the Captain telling how just before the Yalta meeting (between Churchill, Roosevelt and Stalin in February 1945) the Soviet authorities set up a special shop full of groceries, which was only opened long enough to impress a visiting American admiral. The richest examples of Solzhenitsyn's depiction of Soviet window-dressing are to be found in *The First Circle*, where he is especially keen to parade foreigners' gullibility when presented with it.

Some of the wrangling over the text of the work might now seem to be rather precious, given the impact that the *Novy mir* text, cut first by the author of his own volition before submission, and then again under pressure/advice from editors and others, eventually had. Implicit in our closer examination of the authorised version will be the contention that the text is so carefully wrought that only marginal tampering was at all possible. *Ivan Denisovich* survived the Soviet editorial process with as much dignity and integrity as its hero survived his day of forced labour.

The publication of the work in the Soviet Union spawned no less than five different English translations (six, if we count the Soviet-published version of the Parker translation), all, with one exception (Gillon Aitken's version,1970), more or less simultaneously (see Bibliography). Of these, the Hingley/Hayward and the Parker are reckoned to be the most satisfactory. But these too have their shortcomings, and anyway, they were all superseded by the Willetts version of 1991, which is the only one to be based on the Paris text. Given the imprimatur of the bilingual American scholar Alexis Klimoff, himself enjoying the full confidence of Solzhenitsyn, this may be regarded as the authorised English-language edition.

Without going into stylistic questions in detail at this stage, we should note provisionally that the language of *Ivan Denisovich*, demanding enough for foreign readers, is by no means straightforward for native Russians. It was even more demanding for those Russians who encountered the text in 1962, force-fed as they had been for three decades and more on Soviet jargon, both rhetorical and puritanical. Soviet dictionaries were prescriptive and expurgatory. Soviet writers had been obliged to adopt bland linguistic norms, and an enormous gulf had developed between the language of the street and that of the media.

Immediacy and authenticity are two of the key qualities of *Ivan Denisovich*. These and the difficulty of conveying them in translation can be glimpsed even in the title of the work. The working title *Shch-854* (*Odin den' odnogo zeka*) shows Solzhenitsyn at his most compact – too compact for a wide audience. The serial number would convey nothing to readers who had not been in labour camps, and the word *zek* (a phonetic rendition of the abbreviation *z/k*, short for *zakliuchënnyi*, 'convict') did not figure in Soviet dictionaries. However, *Shch* being the 27th letter of the Russian alphabet, plus three digits added on, would very soon give even the least numerate of readers an impression of how many thousands of prisoners there would be in the camp. At the same time, the repetition of *odin* in the parenthesis would convey a notion of inescapability and routine, but by using chilling understatement to do so. Denoting a human being simply by a number would also of course dehumanise him. Such a literary device – but in Solzhenitsyn's work taken very much from real life – would be known, prior to *Ivan Denisovich*, only to that tiny handful of intellectuals who might have come across Zamyatin's science fiction novel *We*, banned in the Soviet Union from the moment it was written (in 1920) until 1988.

Odin den' Ivana Denisovicha would translate literally as 'A Day of Ivan Denisovich', 'Ivan Denisovich's Day', 'One Day of Ivan Denisovich' or 'Ivan Denisovich's One Day'. The now universal English rendition 'One Day in the Life of *Ivan Denisovich*' is certainly pleasing to anglophone ears, but is more leisurely than the original. More importantly, the use of the first name and patronymic, which in Russian connotes the very human qualities of respect, affection and individual dignity, is bound to be lost.

Of the various original translators who sought to render Solzhenitsyn's taut prose into comprehensible English, Hayward and Hingley, with the aid, solicited or otherwise, of an American style-editor, were arguably the most successful. They aimed for an American, or at least mid-Atlantic, register that caught the coarseness, and particularly to British ears, the 'strangeness' of the original. Ralph Parker's version, for many years the one most widely available in Britain, struck many who knew Russian as being far too bland, and even when it first appeared, somewhat dated. The Willetts translation is a vast improvement. The following discussion of two instances of his version are in no way intended to denigrate the translator's efforts, but rather to illustrate how disadvantaged is the English monoglot reader. Here is the opening of the story:

> В пять часов утра, как всегда, пробило подъём — молотком об рэльс у штабного барака. Перерывистый звон слабо прошёл сквозь стёкла, намёрзшие в два пальца, и скоро затих: холодно было, и надзирателю и неохота была долго рукой махать.
>
> Звон утих, а за окном всё так же, как и среди ночи, когда Шухов вставал к параше, была тьма и тьма, да попадало в окно три жёлтых фонаря: два — на зоне, один — внутри лагеря.
>
> И барака что-то не шли отпирать, и не слыхать было, чтобы дневальные брали бочку парашную на палки — выносить.
>
> Шухов никогда не просыпал подъёма, всегда вставал по нему — до развода было часа полтора времени своего, не казённого, и кто знает лагерную жизнь, всегда может подработать.

In the authorised translation the first sentence is cut in two ('The hammer banged reveille on the rail outside camp HQ at five o'clock as always. Time to get up'), arguably making *Ivan Denisovich*'s, or the narrator's, thought processes more grammatical than they actually are. *Pereryvistyi* is rendered as 'ragged', a neat metaphorical touch for an epithet that is usually quite neutral, and more commonly translated as 'intermittent'. The last sentence of the first paragraph might be more literally rendered as: 'It was cold, and the warder had no wish to wave [or 'swing'] his arm for a long time.' The authorised version has: 'Too cold for the warder to go on hammering.' The second paragraph, again, makes two sentences out of one: 'The jangling stopped. Outside it was...', and then goes on to become quite a bit freer than some would like: 'Outside it was still as dark as when Shukhov had got up in the night to use the bucket – pitch black, except for three yellow lights visible from the window...'. One notes in passing that *parasha* is a prison slang term for the slop bucket, and – presumably by olfactory extension or because it denotes the location where toilet gossip begins – it also means 'a rumour'. The word order in the final paragraph ('*chasa poltora*') suggests approximation ('about an hour and a half') which the English dispenses with here; and the full connotations of *kazënnyi* (a word likewise dispensed with in Willetts' rendition) are lost. This thoroughly pre-Revolutionary term survived with a vengeance into the Soviet era, originally meaning 'fiscal' and later 'State-owned', and simply 'official', 'bureaucratic'; a secondary meaning is 'banal' or 'undistinguished'. The original Russian here sets up a sharper distinction between Ivan's private life and the State's demands than an English translation can fully capture, and perhaps it even hints that the Soviet system is just as bureaucratic and repressive as was the Tsarist one. The reference in this last paragraph to 'camp life' (*lagernaia zhizn'*) is omitted in the translation, though perhaps with good reason. *Lager'* can mean any sort of camp (holiday, young pioneer, political, military), and the burden of these opening paragraphs is to keep the reader somewhat mystified and ill at ease: where can this setting be? To use the word 'camp' straight off in the English translation would perhaps be to give the game away too quickly.

At the end of the working day Ivan and Senka have stayed behind to finish the job and they incur the wrath of all the other prisoners, who are anxious to get back to the relative warmth of the camp:

> Запалились, как собаки бешеные, только слышно: хы-хы! хы-хы!
> Ну, да бригадир на вахте, объяснит же.
> Вот прямо на толпу бегут, страшно.
> Сотни глоток сразу как заулюлюкали: и в мать их, и в отца, и в рот, и в нос, и в ребро. Как пятьсот человек на тебя разъярятся – ещё б не страшно! (p.77)

Leaving aside the over-riding issue of the story's narrative mode, which we address elsewhere and which presents special problems, the two major stumbling blocks here for the translator, as in numerous other instances in the text, are the onomatopoeia and the obscenities. It will be useful to consider in passing the Ralph Parker translation here as well.

Parker has:

> They panted like mad dogs. All you could hear was their hoarse breathing.
> Well, Tiurin was at the gates. He'd explain.
> They were running straight into the crowd. Frightening it was.
> Hundreds of throats booing you at once, and cursing you up hill and down dale. Wouldn't *you* be scared if you had five hundred men blowing off their tops at you?
>
> (pp. 92-3)

The authorised translation, by Harry Willetts, has:

> Shukhov and Senka were as hot as rabid dogs. Their own panting was all they could hear.
> Still, the foreman was at the guard house, he'd explain.
> They were running straight toward the crowd, and it was scary.
> Hundreds of raucous voices started baying at them: cursing them up and down and calling them all the bastards in

> creation. Who wouldn't be scared with five hundred furious
> men yelling at him!   (p. 94)

It is interesting that both translators seek to answer the time-honoured complaint from English readers of Russian fiction that the proper names are so confusing. Parker dispenses with Tyurin's rank and uses his surname, while Willetts names the two belated prisoners: the Russian text does not even supply the personal pronoun, thus pointing up the speed with which they are running and the colloquial idiom in which they express themselves. Both translations wisely eschew any attempt to reproduce exactly in English the onomatopoeic *khy-khy*. Parker's translation of *zapalilis'* is simply wrong, while his 'booing' would seem more appropriate to a dissatisfied audience at a talent contest than to a mob of half-starved, frozen prisoners. Similarly, his rendition of the actual expletives the prisoners use is precious to the point of hilarity. Willetts makes a much better job of it here, but still the underlying coarseness is masked. The Russian text hardly mitigates it by omitting the verb *ebat'* ('to fuck'). The use of interjections like *da* and *zhe* together with the elliptical grammar generally make for a cinematographic and dramatic quality. The coarse colloquialism for 'throat' (*glotka*) is difficult to convey in English.

This discussion of just two brief extracts, chosen more or less at random, provides us with an inkling of the quality of Solzhenitsyn's prose. It is a high-octane mixture which seeks to introduce the reader to an alien land. The last thing it aims to do is immunise against culture shock – as even the most accomplished of translations is fated to do.

II. An Overview of Critical Responses

In charting the reactions to Solzhenitsyn's novel no attempt will be made to detail the purely emotional responses of individual readers, or the more outlandish constructions that were placed on the 'Solzhenitsyn phenomenon' by some fanciful foreign commentators and interpreters. By and large, we will restrict ourselves to the more measured and analytical discussions that the work produced. One needs also to bear in mind that any considered, 'scientific' (*nauchnyi*) literary criticism that Soviet scholars might have felt moved to undertake would have been quickly nipped in the bud, given Solzhenitsyn's rapid fall from official grace. The fullest discussions of *Ivan Denisovich* appeared first of all in the West, and no doubt they were well-intentioned; it is up to the reader of this volume to judge how valid they were.

Responses in the Soviet Union

It was standard Soviet practice, when publishing a work that was at all *risqué*, to attach an explanatory note, a Preface or Afterword, not so much in the spirit of paperback 'blurb' in the West, whose *raison d'être* is to catch the casual browser's eye, but rather to offer a 'correct' interpretation of a work, which might otherwise not get through the censorship, or if it did, might be, in the eyes of the authorities, 'misconstrued' by the 'untutored' reader. A good many ideologically suspect works, often foreign, were thus smuggled through to the Soviet reader by well-intentioned, but curiously schizophrenic Soviet editors. This was the background to Tvardovsky's Preface to the first publication of *Ivan Denisovich*. One should add that the Preface was submitted to Khrushchev along with the story proper. Solzhenitsyn was unhappy about such an introduction, preferring to let the text speak for itself. None the less, Tvardovsky's words set the tone for the other official Soviet responses.

The main tenor of these reviews was of course political – the message being that the breaches of Soviet legality which Solzhenitsyn describes were now a thing of the past, but we must all be acquainted with them so that they might never occur again, and that the publication of Solzhenitsyn's book was fully in line with the position set out by Nikita Khrushchev at the 22nd Party Congress; the author's artistry was such that it conveyed a hitherto unacknowledged truth with great power; Soviet writers could now tackle any subject. The discussion of Solzhenitsyn's artistic method was on the whole general, rather than detailed, and any great philosophical truths which one cared to discern in the work were referred to blandly. Any orthodox reader or critic would have no trouble at this level in defining *Ivan Denisovich* in terms of Socialist Realism.

Tvardovsky's piece was entitled 'Instead of a Foreword', perhaps a veiled confession that what he was saying could hardly do justice to the work, as well as a hint of prescience that the discussion over *Ivan Denisovich* was not going to be short-lived. It opens:

> The vital material (*zhiznennyi material*) at the basis of A. Solzhenitsyn's novella is unusual in Soviet literature. It carries within itself an echo of the unhealthy (or 'painful' – *boleznennyi*) phenomena in our development associated with the period of the cult of personality – now exposed and rejected by the Party – which though they are not so very far behind us in terms of time, seem to us as the distant past. But whatever the past was like, it must never become a matter of indifference for the present. The guarantee of a full and irrevocable break with everything in the past which clouded it is to be found in the truthful, courageous and complete comprehension of its consequences.[1]

He went on to quote from Khrushchev's speech at the 22nd Party Congress to the effect that it was a duty to investigate thoroughly everything connected with the abuse of power, and 'Time will pass, we will all die, we are all mortal, but while we continue to work, we can and must explain a great deal and tell the truth to the Party and the people'; and this must be done, according to Khrushchev, so that the mistakes of the past will never be repeated. Having invoked the First Secretary, Tvardovsky then fastened on to qualities in the work that would, in the eyes of any conformist critic, hardly distinguish it from a host of prize-winning sagas about the Civil War or the Five-Year Plans:

> The undoubted victory of the artist is in the fact that this bitterness and pain have nothing in common with a feeling of hopeless oppression. On the contrary, the impression one is left with by this book, so unusual in its unembellished and harsh truth, is that it somehow liberates the soul from the unutterability of that which has to be uttered, and thus strengthens in the soul feelings both courageous and lofty.

Later Tvardovsky produces a neat synthesis of what could be called political correctness and literary insight:

> This novella allows us to draw one more simple and instruc-
> tive conclusion: the genuinely significant subject matter, its
> fidelity to life's great truth, its profound humanity in its
> approach to the depiction of even the most difficult subjects
> cannot help but summon to life a corresponding form. In *One
> Day* this is bright and original in the very humdrum routine
> it portrays and in its external undemandingness, it is less than
> anything concerned with itself and is therefore filled with
> inner dignity and strength.

Stripped of the ponderous Soviet jargon, what this boils down to is that
Solzhenitsyn's novel tells an *a priori* truth, and does so in such an original
and graphic form that all readers – not just the Soviet dispossessed – can
relate to it, and that [like all serious works of art? R.P.] it is spiritually
invigorating. Moreover, it implies – as we have suggested earlier – that form
and content in the work are indivisible, and in this sense it is impossible to
emasculate it or tone it down seriously. Tvardovsky rounds off his Preface
with a warning-cum-apology for any fastidious taste that might be outraged
by the occasional coarseness of expression typical of the novel's setting.
Above all, the editor concludes, we feel a sense of gratitude to the author,
which he hopes other readers will share.

Two 'heavyweight' reviews came hard on the heels of publication:
Konstantin Simonov, a respected author of Second World War novels,
wrote an effusive notice for *Izvestia* (18 November 1962), using a phrase
that was subsequently much quoted – in his view 'Solzhenitsyn has shown
himself to be a true helper of the Party'. Vladimir Ermilov, a long-serving
and staunchly establishment critic, struck a similarly eulogistic note in
Pravda (23 November 1962). Again emphasising the truth that the work
conveyed, he referred to the 20th and 22nd Party Congresses and the cult
of personality. He also drew a parallel between Solzhenitsyn and Tolstoy,
and went on to call the work 'epic'. Here was literary comment, albeit brief,
which was worth reflecting on.

There was an element of stage-management in these reviews and both of
them, together with Tvardovsky's Preface, stressed the link between the
Party line and Solzhenitsyn's message. Grigory Baklanov, like Simonov, a
writer of Second World War stories, went a good deal further in his review
for *Literaturnaya gazeta* (22 November 1962), making the memorable, and
as it turned out somewhat ironical, declaration that it was now 'impossible
to go on writing as one did before'. A good many Soviet writers, Baklanov
included, did – after the heady days of the early 1960s – continue to write
as they had done before. However, Baklanov was absolutely right in that
Solzhenitsyn had stirred the intelligentsia's and the nation's conscience to
such an extent that unpleasant truths could no longer be so easily swept
under the carpet.

Ivan Denisovich impelled thousands of readers to write to the press or directly to the author, and it became clear that the whole Soviet system was shaken. People at the very top began to take fright, and this was reflected in the 'literary' debates surrounding the work. Lakshin writes that 'After some extravagant praise (V. Ermilov wrote in *Pravda* that it was a work 'of Tolstoyan power'), there was a gradual switch to abuse of Solzhenitsyn in the press and at writers' meetings, at first in fairly restrained and oblique manner, but then month by month the attacks grew fiercer and more malicious.'[2] One notes that at first Solzhenitsyn's name had been linked in various quarters with those of all the great Russian writers, but that the perception of this linkage eventually turned from positive to negative. Solzhenitsyn became accused of 'archaism' and, through his hero, of 'karataevshchina' (Karataev being the meek, benevolent peasant who appears towards the end of *War and Peace*) in particular. I. Chicherov came to write that 'Indeed, at times one detects something Karataevan and servile in his [Ivan Denisovich's] reflections, something which is also evident in his behaviour, only perhaps without the Karataevan characteristic of consoling others', and he goes on to regret that Solzhenitsyn did not develop the characters of Buynovsky and Yu-81 as a kind of counterweight.[3]

The critic who had been so supportive in the publication of the work sprang to its defence. In January 1964 *Novy mir* published his article 'Ivan Denisovich, His Friends and Foes'.[4] By now, there was circulating the highly instructive anecdote 'Tell me what you think of *One Day* and I'll tell you who you are'.

Lakshin's lengthy article, which in turn spawned a good number of counter-attacks, is worthy of close attention on several counts. Firstly, it offered a detailed discussion of the hero and some of the other key characters and scenes, as it were quite simply reminding the reader of what the original text consisted of. It would not be too much to say that *Ivan Denisovich* was by now fast becoming a symbol, a rallying point, for warring factions and that what it was actually about and what it actually said did not matter too much in some quarters. Secondly, Lakshin's article provided an overview of and a response to some of Solzhenitsyn's chief detractors. Thirdly, it still stands today as a fine example of liberal Soviet literary criticism, which as such was obliged to couch its arguments using the requisite terminology and making at least some reference to literary figures respected by the Soviet establishment.

Lakshin reminds the reader that the work only appeared just over a year before and already had become a 'socio-political event'.[5] Some of Solzhenitsyn's opponents went unnamed in the article – like the one who argued that it was easy for Solzhenitsyn to write his story because the author equalled Ivan Denisovich and all Solzhenitsyn had to do was describe his own experiences. Lakshin tells us that this may be flattering for the author, but it is a naive and unjust remark. It certainly is, given that Solzhenitsyn was at pains to create a thoroughly unintellectual hero and was always unhappy at those critics who suggested that his book would have been improved if he had chosen an intellectual as the main protagonist. Lakshin reiterates the view that the work conveys graphically the truth and that Solzhenitsyn's artistic courage resided in his studious refusal to create some kind of 'intrigue' – on the contrary, his aim was 'strict, simple, almost ascetic'. He then made a point that was to be echoed by a good deal of Western criticism later on:

> Solzhenitsyn disappointed those people who were expecting from him a story about evil-doings, tortures and bloody torments, about the excesses of inhumanity in the camp, about the martyrs and heroes of hard labour. It is a strange thing to confess, but the first impression that we experienced, when we started to read the story, was: even there people live. Even there they work, sleep, eat, quarrel and make up, even there they take delight in little things (*raduiutsia malym radostiam*), they hope, they argue, occasionally they joke at one another...[6]

He quotes the opening words of the story which 'fall, weightily, heavily, as if hacked off' and tells us that Solzhenitsyn has us 'see and recognise the life of a *zek* not from the side, but from within, "from him"'. Shukhov 'lives in those special conditions, when all things and relations acquire a different value from their usual one'. There is in the story 'as it were, a whole lexicon of the details of camp everyday life (*byt*), described by the artist with socio-ethnographic exactitude, and in all probability anyone who writes about this after Solzhenitsyn will willy-nilly have to follow in his footsteps.'[7] A lesser artist than Solzhenitsyn would have elected to write about the worst day and the worst time in Ivan Denisovich's life. Lakshin also refers to the work as 'epic',[8] without going into any explanation of the term, and concludes his introduction, without being able to speak for other readers, with reflections as to what he was doing on that day in January 1951 when Ivan Denisovich was building his wall. (Apart from the more frivolous things that a student might be doing then, he was, as it happens, mugging up on Stalin's recently published study of language – incidentally, an academic achievement of the dictator's much ridiculed in *The First Circle*.) Lakshin then went on to take issue with certain critics he felt had expressed negative views of *Ivan Denisovich*, delineating two time-honoured critical methods – what he called the normative and the analytical. Briefly, he argued that the first method involved the critic coming to a given work with a set of preconceived notions and then judging the work against them. The analytical method consisted, by contrast, in approaching a work as a reflection of a life that was 'vital, contradictory and constantly changing', drawing on the testimony of the artist and reaching a judgement about the work itself and the life that it depicted.

L. Fomenko (in *Literaturnaya Rossiia*, January 11, 1963) stated that although the work expressed a cruel and bitter truth it had not 'risen to the philosophy of the time, to a broad generalisation capable of embracing the opposing phenomena of the epoch'.[9] This somewhat disparaging remark was challenged in the same publication a week later by L. Lomidze who argued that one could not demand of an author that he grasp the ungraspable (*ob" iat' neob"iatnoe*) and pointed out that Solzhenitsyn had written not a *roman-epopeia*, but only a little novella: 'As if it were possible in one day in the life of a convict to grasp the dialectics of all the connections, struggles and contradictions of the epoch!'. Lakshin refutes the notion here that *Ivan Denisovich* is limited in scope by discussing the rich diversity of characters in the book, which presented us with a world that was 'many-sided, vital, with an abundance of connections, qualities, relationships,' which did not allude only to the specifics 'of the labour camp theme'.[10]

Other critics, Lakshin complained, had been denigrating Solzhenitsyn in pin-pricking fashion by comparing/contrasting his work with others that were clearly lightweight (for example, I. Lazutin's novel *The Police Sergeant*). N. Sergovantsev, writing in the conservative *Oktyabr'* (no. 4, 1963, entitled 'The Tragedy of Solitude and "Utter Routine Life" [*sploshnoi byt*]'), had been more specifically disparaging. In his view Ivan Denisovich's 'spiritual world is extremely limited, his intellectual life is of no particular interest' while conceding that the hero is still an interesting character. In Sergovantsev's opinion, he is interesting because being an ordinary, average *(riadovoi)* man he ought, according to all that life and Soviet literature have taught us, be a fighter – he should protest against and resist the tragic circumstances in which he finds himself. Yet, Sergovantsev states, he 'subjugates himself body and soul' to them, and there is not the 'slightest inner protest, no hint of a desire to realise the reasons for his difficult situation, not even an attempt to find out about them from more knowledgeable people'.[11] And he asks how there can be any firmness of character (*stoikost'*) in the hero when all he is concerned with is survival, an extra bowl of skilly, earning a bit on the side, trying to keep warm. The critic concludes that Ivan has inherited the traits of his personality not from the Soviet people of the 1930s and 40s, but from the 'patriarchal peasant' *(patriarkhal'nyi muzhichok)*, and asserts that 'Ivan Denisovich cannot lay claim to the role of "national type of our epoch (*narodnyi tip nashei epokhi*)"'.

So now, in some quarters, Solzhenitsyn was not so much 'a true helper of the Party' as the creator of a pre-Revolutionary docile and subservient peasant. Sergovantsev attempts a coup de grâce with references to Solzhenitsyn's other published works (*Matryona's Home* and *Incident at Krechetovka Station*) and his declaration that 'a truly artistic work opens up life's boundless horizons' for the reader, and this is just what Solzhenitsyn does not do. Lakshin retorts that *Ivan Denisovich* in fact bears witness to the democratisation of literature since the 20th Party Congress and that during the cult of personality writers were more interested in what went on at meetings of the collective farm management than what went on under the roofs of the villagers' huts.[12] He accuses Sergovantsev of blackening Ivan Denisovich and denying him any *narodnost'* [a key quality in any work of Socialist Realism, the term might be translated variously as 'nationality', 'national character' or 'folk character', R.P.].

Lakshin then goes on to a detailed discussion of Ivan's qualities, his past life in his village, the way he values specific things in the camp, and how he has 'chosen a life'[13] that for all its vicissitudes is a cut above sponging off others or being a stool pigeon. For Lakshin 'Shukhov has such inner firmness (*ustoichivost'*), faith in himself, in his hands and his mind (or 'reason' – *razum*), that he does not even need God' and thus he differs from the patriarchal peasant, for such irreligious traits were 'formed and strengthened during the years of Soviet power'. For Lakshin, Ivan comes into his own during the brick-laying scene 'and to pass by these pages would mean failing to understand the chief thing about Ivan Denisovich. I cannot remember when or even if we have read in our prose such a poetic and inspired description of simple manual work; the author so immerses us in its rhythm and harmony, that you seem yourself to feel the straining of the muscles, and the difficulty, and the weariness, and the amiable zeal of the work, and the concerted excitement (*druzhnyi azart*)'.[14] Lakshin goes on to contrast Solzhenitsyn's abilities here with those on display in standard 'production novels', where the hero's personal life is divorced from the description of the work process and the result is 'intolerably tedious'.

According to Lakshin the novel is optimistic and implies that truth will triumph over injustice. The hero's work is one of his supports, but another is his relationships with other people, and Lakshin tells us that the second hero, after Ivan, is the work team, and that we find in the novel a 'pride in common, collective work' (*obshchii, kollektivnyi*),[15] and he points out instances of Ivan's regard for others and theirs for him (e.g. when Senka waits for him after they are late finishing their shift, so that, if necessary, they can face the music together). Lakshin's remarks here are designed to rebut those critics who detected individualism or solitude in the hero. Similarly, Lakshin sees the fact that Ivan is not an 'ideal hero' in the eyes of some as an artistic strength, not a weakness – Solzhenitsyn's worthiness as an artist resides 'precisely in the fact that there is no pseudo-folky sentimentalisation [a difficult phrase to put into English here – *psevdonarodnicheskoe sentimental'nichanie*, R.P.], forced idealisation even of those characters whom he loves, whose tragedy he sympathises with'.

I. Chicherov's examination of *Ivan Denisovich,* entitled 'In The Name Of The Future' (*Moskovskaya pravda*, December 8, 1962), drew particular fire from Lakshin. Chicherov was especially unhappy about the uncomprehending attitude of the peasant hero Ivan to the intellectuals in the piece. He felt that the novel could have been improved if Solzhenitsyn had developed further the characters of Buynovsky and the 'tall old man', who in Chicherov's view may not have been a communist but was an intellectual; Chicherov writes: 'In my view the real shortcoming of the novella is that this intellectual and moral tragedy of those people who think sharply, and not just about the "trouble" that's befallen them, but also about how and why it all happened, is not revealed'. For 'trouble' Chicherov uses, in inverted commas, the dialect form *biada* (instead of *beda*) in the way that Ivan Denisovich might, thus underlining his dissatisfaction with Solzhenitsyn's uneducated hero. Chicherov is exercised by the manner in which the hero perceives the intellectuals in the story, and he detects, behind the thought processes of Ivan, Solzhenitsyn's own 'ironic and sometimes even contemptuous attitude towards such people'.[16]

Lakshin rejects entirely the way that Chicherov distinguishes between intellectuals and ordinary folk, claiming that it smacks of an old and vulgar (*poshlyi*) prejudice. For Lakshin, *Ivan Denisovich* makes a distinction not between intellectuals and ordinary folk, but between hardworking people on the one hand, and conscious or unconscious parasites on the other. He notes that nearly all the reviews of the book make mention of the scene where Tsezar and the prisoner Kh-123 are arguing about Eisenstein. Here there are indeed some pithy comments about art, and they are all the more arresting for being made by two inmates of a labour camp, where one would expect the struggle for material existence to banish any such refinement. But Lakshin informs us that few commentators note that there is a third figure present during the discussion – Ivan Denisovich, who meekly reminds them of his presence, wants to linger in the warm surroundings and is to all intents and purposes ignored by Tsezar, when he hands Tsezar his *kasha*. Lakshin sees Tsezar here not merely being defeated in the argument about art, but more importantly by the way he takes the bowl from Ivan. We suddenly feel hostility towards this otherwise sympathetic and polite character, though Lakshin goes on to say that his selfishness is such that it inspires more a smile in us than ill-feeling or indignation. Lakshin sees a similarity between Tsezar and the carpet painters back in Ivan's village of Temgenyovo; and he perceives more of a similarity between Ivan and Captain Buynovsky than between Tsezar and Buynovsky, even though these two are, unlike Ivan, of the intelligentsia.

So Lakshin has little time for those who saw in Solzhenitsyn's work a disparagement of the intelligentsia and who bemoaned the fact that the peasant hero seemed to understand so little about his predicament and the reasons for it. He had even less time for at least one attempt, in fictional form, to provide an alternative picture of life in Stalin's camps, one which sought to exonerate the trusties (*pridurki*). Lakshin writes: 'The attitude of

Shukhov to the trusties is exactly the same as his perplexity as regards the light industry of the carpet painters, it has at its base a people's (*narodnyi*) attitude towards work and towards the moral duty that people working together have towards one another.'[17] The story which so incensed Lakshin was Boris Dyakov's *Perezhitoe*, much praised by *Oktyabr'*, and in Lakshin's view little more than a polemic against *Ivan Denisovich*. The story argued that trusties were simply 'clever convicts' and that though there were victims of illegality in the camps there were also some 'real villains'.

Lakshin rounds off his article with a ringing endorsement of Solzhenitsyn's work, re-emphasising its *narodnost'*, and linking his name with some of the classical writers of the nineteenth century: Nekrasov, Shchedrin, Tolstoy and Chekhov. Moreover, as socialist legality and Leninist norms were now being re-established, such works as *Ivan Denisovich* had the support of the Party, as Ilyichev (head of the ideological commission on the Central Committee) had stated. In sum:

> Solzhenitsyn has written this novella because he could not help but write it. He wrote it as people fulfil their duty – without any concessions to falsehood, with complete candour and direct-ness. And so his book, for all the brutality of its subject matter, has become a Party book (*stala partiinoi knigoi*), fighting for the ideals of the people and the Revolution.[18]

Lakshin's defence of *Ivan Denisovich*, much abbreviated here, for the most part relies on an examination of the text, and he offers some astute insights. Yet one notes that he has to bill the work as one that is both *narodnyi* and, in the end, *partiinyi*, i.e. one that has at least two of the essential ingredients of a Socialist Realist work (*partiinost'*, 'Party-mindedness', first coined by Lenin in his article 'Party Organisation and Party Literature' of 1905, being the most important). It is also worth noting that the entire polemic around the novel seemed to be conducted in terms of whether, crudely, it 'told the truth, the whole truth and nothing but the truth', what the moral standing of the various characters was, and what it could teach us. Soviet aesthetics, even at their most liberal, would not, or could not, rise to anything more sophisticated than this. Some Western critics might take the view that indeed Solzhenitsyn himself does not rise to anything more sophisticated, that his moral vision is too simplistic and his artistic method traditional, even out-dated. Other Western critics were to warm to Solzhenitsyn's 'old-fashioned' and clear-cut moral perceptions.

Before taking these questions further, we should consider one other major contribution to the discussions on *Ivan Denisovich*, which appeared in the Soviet Union. In 1965 the academic journal *Voprosy kul'tury rechi*[19] carried a detailed article examining the language and style of Solzhenitsyn's work, and in so doing it represented a clear exception to the other Soviet responses. In this article Tatyana Vinokur identified the chief features of

Solzhenitsyn's style and responded to some of the complaints that had been
raised about the author's use of language. She took as a starting point Lev
Tolstoy's utterance to the effect that a work of literature had to contain 'the
only possible order of the only possible words'. Solzhenitsyn, in Vinokur's
words, 'set himself a complicated stylistic task' for he had merged into one
the image of the author and the hero and therefore had to create a linguistic
'mask' which would combine: '1. the individual peculiarities of the hero's
speech corresponding to his character, 2. the broader features of the dialect
of his native village of Temgenyovo (or more precisely – the general
characteristics of the dialectal-popular (*dialektno-prostorechnyi*) "speaking" characteristic of the contemporary peasant) and 3. the speech colouring
of his environment as a prisoner'.[20]

Vinokur cites several instances where the text slips seamlessly from
direct speech to an authorial viewpoint or *vice versa*, sometimes within a
single sentence. A good example is when Ivan, on his way back to the camp,
sees the other column of men from the engineering works (p. 86 in the
authorised Russian text, pp.105-6 of the Willetts translation). The English
version falls short of the original on a number of counts here. It combines
three paragraphs into one. The sentence 'They would walk a few paces –
and start running again' is set out separately in the original; and the shift in
narrative viewpoint is lost entirely: the one-sentence paragraph, which
Vinkur quotes, is as follows:

> Как хвост на холм вывалил, так и Шухов увидел: справа от
> них, далеко в степи, чернелась ещё колонна, шла она нашей
> колонне наперекос и, должно быть увидав, тоже припустила.

The translation has:

> When the tail-end reached the hilltop Shukhov saw to their
> right, some distance away on the steppe, another black
> column on the move. The others must have spotted this
> column and speeded up to cut across its path.

Apart from some of the speed being lost in the translation by breaking
up the original into separate sentences, the whole notion of 'our' column,
with all the hero's own thought processes and his notions of solidarity and
team spirit, are swept away.

Vinokur argues that the style of *Ivan Denisovich* results from 'the
peculiar use of the interconnected possibilities of *skaz*, of the shifts in
authorial and direct narration and the special qualities of colloquial speech'.[21]
She also identifies defamiliarisation (*ostranenie*) as an occasional feature,[22]
whereby the reader is made to see something from a new and unexpected

angle. Vinokur does not discuss *skaz* as such to any degree – as a common term in Russian literary studies, it perhaps needs no exegesis. But for English students some explanation would perhaps not go amiss, since Solzhenitsyn's modified use of the device in his story is crucial to an appreciation of the work. Strictly speaking, *skaz* involves telling a story in the language of one of the participants in the story; it is the author using *chuzhoi iazyk*, i.e. someone else's language. Frequently, the purpose of *skaz* is to create a comic, irreverent and/or incompetent narrator – Zoshchenko's short stories contain some fine examples. In *Ivan Denisovich* the *skaz* technique has been adapted, though. For one thing, Ivan does not *say* very much; rather, he observes, thinks, recalls and reacts. Solzhenitsyn often reports Ivan's mental and emotional world in Ivan's own words, thus *skaz* blends with a thoroughly coherent 'stream of consciousness'.

Roy Pascal has made a thorough study of the device, which in French literary studies is known as 'style indirecte libre'. In Pascal's view, it is through this device that 'the imagination and the irony of the narrator' are revealed and 'we hear in "style indirecte libre" a dual voice, which, through vocabulary, sentence structure, and intonation subtly fuses the two voices of the character and the narrator'.[23] One might add that although Pascal's wide-ranging study does address Russian literature, he is less at home here. Consequently, he perhaps misses the point that the sequence of tenses in Russian, more so than in French, German or English, is actually *predisposed* towards the dual voice.

Here then, through the adapted form of *skaz*, the 'dual voice', we have the chief buttress of the qualities in *Ivan Denisovich*, which we noted earlier: immediacy and authenticity. Consequently, Ivan is far from being the comic and incompetent narrator one usually associates with *skaz*, but rather an educator – he initiates the reader into the ways of camp life. He is a prism through which more than a few characters become objects of his (and the reader's?) condescension, derision, disapproval, or occasionally, sympathy.

The related aspects of Solzhenitsyn's style which Vinokur addresses concern *prostorechie* (popular speech), prison slang and out-and-out vulgarity. Vinokur recalls the views of some readers that the work could have been improved if it had been expurgated, and she mocks them with a few suggestions: instead of *parasha* substitute something like *tualetnaia bochka*, instead of *padly* put *durnye liudi*.[24] It is interesting for non-native speakers of Russian to survey the squabbles among native speakers over Solzhenitsyn's style, and to note some of the connotations that particular turns of phrase might have. Vinokur rightly points out that some of the unfamiliar terminology becomes clear from the context. She also records that, for example, *shmon* (a frisking, search) in Solzhenitsyn's lexicon carries many more connotations of humiliation and discomfort than would the more literary term *obysk*. Vinokur also argues that there are, given the setting of the story, relatively few instances of prison slang – only about 40.[25] Some of the better-known examples she cites are *stuchat'* (to inform), *zanachit'* (to stash) and *dokhodiaga* (a goner), *kum* (camp commandant), and *gulag* — a word that since 1974 and the publication of *The Gulag Archipelago* has, of course, become international.

As regards *prostorechie*, Vinokur reminds us of the, now well-attested, affection that Solzhenitsyn has always had for Dahl's famous dictionary. In Vinokur's opinion Solzhenitsyn neither made words up nor simply lifted them from Dahl – rather, he checked in Dahl what he heard around him, and thus some terms in Solzhenitsyn and Dahl are similar but not identical: for example, in *Ivan Denisovich* we find *doboltki, ziablyi, zakhriastok*, whereas Dahl records *doboltka* (only in the singular), *ziablivyi, zakhriast'e*. However, we should note that Solzhenitsyn's language has caused controversy, and not necessarily politically inspired opposition, sometimes even among émigrés.

Vinokur ends her vigorous defence of Solzhenitsyn's style with some reference to his metaphorical language, at times not overly decorous, with examples like *bushlat dereviannyi* for 'coffin' and *namordnik dorozhnyi*, meaning the cloth that the prisoner would use to shield his face against the wind. She concludes her analysis:

> The laconic result of the hero's gloomy reflections, concen-
> trated in these remarks, is the stylistic key to the whole
> novella, a key which helps the reader discover the work's
> precise truthfulness and its inimitable expressiveness, which
> in literature do not tolerate any linguistic compromises.[26]

Critical Responses in the West

Not unsurprisingly, much of the initial Western critical response to *Ivan Denisovich* was, like the Soviet response, focussed on the raw facts that the story depicted. Any substantive difference that there was resided in the fact that the story simply endorsed, in the eyes of many, what unsympathetic commentators on Soviet affairs had suspected or half-known all along. Such commentators were by no means as keen as Soviet critics were, to see the work as an instrument to exorcise Stalinism once and for all, to reform the Soviet system, to return it to what any 'loyal opposition' in the Soviet Union might call 'Leninist norms'.

One Western critic to argue that one of the work's chief merits lay in its straightforward depiction of a history hitherto unknown was Gleb Zekulin.[1] Zekulin says that of the four stories Solzhenitsyn had thus far published (*Ivan Denisovich, Matryona's Home, An Incident at Krechetovka Station* [in Collected Works, *Incident at Kochetovka Station*], and *For the Good of the Cause*), the first two stand out 'for their informative or cognitive value'. Indeed, in his view, *Ivan Denisovich* is 'a mine of information, much more so than the well-known "Notes from the House of the Dead" by Dostoevski which treats in a not dissimilar artistic manner the same theme – life in a prison camp – and to which it has often been compared'.[2] Zekulin tells us that from Solzhenitsyn's story we learn all about the daily routine in the camp, what the prisoners eat, the punishments they can expect, the lay-out of the camp and of the building site to which they are marched every day. Perhaps of more importance in Zekulin's view is the portrayal of the prisoners, classified roughly into good, hard-working individuals and the bad ones, who contrive to find themselves cushy jobs. The critic quickly goes on to point out the greater subtleties in this categorisation 'good', 'better' and 'not-so-good'. He also notes – contentiously, it could be said, but none the less with some prescience of the debates that were eventually to emerge concerning Solzhenitsyn's nationalist tendencies – 'the possibly unconscious unwillingness on the part of the author to put the non-Russians into the group of the "better ones"; for instance, the two Estonians who work conscientiously, etc., etc., and possess in addition other moral and civic virtues, are nevertheless classified as "not-so-good ones". Is it that Solzhenitsyn, like his nineteenth-century predecessors, still views non-Russians as incapable of entirely pure, unselfish and noble motivations?'.[3]

Zekulin points out that the story also gives us information about the hard life of the free workers who live near the construction site and also about the very harsh conditions on the collective farms, with few able-bodied men remaining there to work, but rather earning big money by stencilling carpet patterns. Zekulin also detects in the work ' a short survey of Soviet history from a peculiar though not unique angle: the generations of camp inmates',[4] saying that the first waves of prisoners came in 1930 with the collectivisation programme, and they never diminished, being followed by the victims of the purges in the wake of Kirov's assassination in 1934, and of the great purge in 1937; and then came those – like Ivan – arrested after having escaped from the Germans during the war. Zekulin rounds off his discussion with remarks on the wall-building scene:

> At first glance this scene is the apotheosis of work, a song of praise to work (and, incidentally, the story's only 're-demption' theme). But, seen more closely, it becomes quite plain that Shukhov and his brigade do not work for the work's sake but in order to erect as quickly as possible a shield against the killing frost and to receive a bigger ration of bread. Their enthusiasm has no other basis. Among his mates Shukhov is the only one who pays any attention to the quality of the work (and even he slips a little towards the end of the scene), and the pride of work well done is a particular feature of his own character, not the general attitude.[5]

There is much that one could take issue with in Zekulin's remarks (for instance, that he makes no distinction between Ivan and Solzhenitsyn), but at the same time he offers some astute insights, concluding his survey of Solzhenitsyn's four stories with the assertion that the author 'might be a great writer'. 'His works are not just reproductions, more or less faithful, of certain characters or incidents. They are probes into human life and gauges of human behaviour. As such, they necessarily preach, teach, and are, ultimately, moralistic.'[6]

Zekulin retains a degree of liberal neutrality in his assessment. But it needs to be borne in mind that Solzhenitsyn, on the strength of *Ivan Denisovich*, was granted membership of the Union of Soviet Writers, and was received by Khrushchev; in 1964, he was a candidate (unsuccessful, as it turned out) for the Lenin Prize for literature. It was natural then that Marxist intellectuals in the West (and elsewhere), as they watched the Soviet Union's attempts at reform (of which Solzhenitsyn was willy-nilly a part), should offer their own interpretation of the author's work. Eventually, nearly all shades of political opinion were to claim Solzhenitsyn's loyalties, and the same was true for particular religious groups. Whatever one's political or religious views may be, perhaps the ultimate test of a work of art's validity is that it defies categorisation and is, if not 'all things to all men', at least 'many things to many men'. It retains its appeal despite the ravages of time and the attempts of given interest groups to hijack it for their own ends. It is a measure of *Ivan Denisovich's* power that, in addition to restoring to millions of semi-literate ex-prisoners a voice and some dignity, it compelled some of the world's leading intellectuals to reach for their pens. Whatever one might think about *Ivan Denisovich*, it is a story that is never going to appear as quaint, dated, abstruse and verbose as some of the comment it generated.

For this reason, if nothing else, the views of Georg Lukács (1885-1971) are worthy of attention. A Hungarian communist philosopher and literary critic, he lived in Russia during the 1930s and the war years, returning to his native Budapest in 1945. In 1956 he was Minister of Culture in the revolutionary government and after arrest and deportation by the Soviet government was allowed in 1957 to return to Hungary. Despite his ideological position he was held in high regard throughout the world for his scholarship. No doubt his attitude towards the Soviet government was as ambivalent as theirs was to him. Thus, Solzhenitsyn's books, artistic, truthful, and enjoying (at least temporarily) official Soviet approval, were a lifeline.

His essay on *Ivan Denisovich* of 1964 was combined with a study of *The First Circle* and *Cancer Ward* (1969) to produce a book which made a prophecy and celebrated the fulfilment of that prophecy. 'The novella frequently appears either as a precursor to a conquest of reality by the great epic and dramatic forms, or as a rearguard, a termination at the end of a period; that is, it appears either in the phase of a Not-Yet (*Nochnicht*) in the artistically universal mastery of the given social world, or in the phase of the No-Longer (*Nichtmehr*)'.[7] Boccaccio precedes the period of the great bourgeois novels (Balzac, Stendhal), Maupassant rounds it off. 'One can say of contemporary and near-contemporary fiction that it often withdraws from the novel into the novella in its attempt to provide truth of man's moral stature', and he cites as examples Conrad's *Typhoon* or *The Shadow Line* and Hemingway's *The Old Man and the Sea*. In the case of Solzhenitsyn, he argues, it is a question of a beginning, 'an exploration of the new reality, and not, as in the works of the important bourgeois writers mentioned, the conclusion of a period'.[8]

Lukács informs us that Socialist Realism (represented by A. Tolstoy, Sholokhov and others) was at its best in the 1920s [before the theory was officially promulgated, R.P.], and degenerated under Stalin in the 1930s into what he calls 'illustrating literature' which grew out of Party resolutions and produced puppet-like characters which were either positive heroes or para-sites.[9] *Ivan Denisovich* represents the rebirth of Socialist Realism, and is 'a significant overture to this process of literary rediscovery of self in the socialist present'.[10] Solzhenitsyn's hero, like, in Lukács's view, the Socialist Realist heroes of the 1920s literature, grows out of the past and is thus as authentic as they were. 'The world of socialism today stands on the eve of a renaissance of Marxism [...] it is also wrong to attempt to give socialist realism a premature burial'.[11] Lukács dwells on the routine in the camp, Solzhenitsyn's extremely economic descriptive method,[12] and asserts that the work acquires a 'symbolic totality'.[13] The critic makes some mention of the three other published stories, but regards *Ivan Denisovich* as the most successful. For our purposes it is sufficient to quote only the opening paragraph of the second part of his book:

> In the previous essay I argued the case that Solzhenitsyn's novellas represent a significant step in the renewal of the great traditions of socialist realism of the nineteen-twenties. The question of whether he himself would bring about the rebirth of socialist realism and its new growth into a significant world literature was one that I cautiously left open. I can now state with pleasure that I was far too cautious: Solzhenitsyn's two new novels represent a new high point in contemporary world literature.[14]

A great many readers would be prepared to agree with the last sentence here. But it is difficult to see, with the benefit of hindsight, the arguments about the rebirth of Socialist Realism, Marxism and so on, as being anything other than convoluted and wrong-headed. Lukács's comments on aspects of Solzhenitsyn's texts are often acute and sound (certainly there are affinities with Hemingway, Conrad, Tolstoy and others), but in his excitement at the artistry in the novels, Lukács has overlooked the simple fact that they were both banned in the Soviet Union and that their author was about to be expelled from the Writers' Union. Moreover, of course, Lukács did not live long enough to see the object of his admiration expelled from the Soviet Union, or the collapse of the Soviet Union and of Marxism as preached (and practised?) there. Neither was he to witness the increasingly religious and nationalist sentiments that Solzhenitsyn came to exhibit.

Curiously enough, there are arguments to support the view of Solzhenitsyn as a Socialist Realist – but only by ditching all the verbiage and taking the position that Socialist Realism is achieved when the 'message' (socialist, capitalist, liberal, religious or whatever) in a given work outweighs its artistry, when it tries to direct the reader's imagination instead of stimulating it. Thus, *For the Good of the Cause* could, without too much difficulty, be billed as Socialist Realism; and indeed, lumpen readers of a left-wing bent and deprived of Lukács's erudition, did – after their initial honeymoon with Solzhenitsyn and what they perceived as the moral rejuvenation of Marxism – dismiss the author as a kind of anti-Socialist Realist, i.e. an instrument of Western anti-Soviet propaganda. In any event, it would not be difficult to find passages in some of Solzhenitsyn's books (not *Ivan Denisovich*, this author would argue) where the propaganda looms unpalatably large. The same can be said of Charles Dickens.

The eminent American literary scholar Irving Howe was one of several critics to challenge Lukács. Reminding his readers of Lukács's equivocation over the years, he suggests that the Marxist critic has actually identified in Solzhenitsyn qualities that are so lacking in himself, primarily 'independence' and 'courage', but buttressed by a clear-cut moral awareness. Howe notes, as does Lukács, Solzhenitsyn's (and Pasternak's) penchant for the anti-modernist, nineteenth-century realistic novel; but unlike Lukács, he does not attribute this to 'a deliberate or ideological rejection of literary modernism'. In Howe's view, such an approach rests instead on:

> moral-political grounds [...] a persuasion that genuinely to return to the Tolstoyan novel, which the Stalinist dogma of 'socialist realism' had celebrated in words but caricatured in performance, would constitute a revolutionary act of the spirit. It would signify a struggle for human renewal, for the reaffirmation of the image of a free man as that image can excite our minds beyond all ideological decrees.[15]

In discussing *The First Circle* and *Cancer Ward* Lukács detected a weakness in the author in that his good characters were 'plebeian' rather than politically and socially aware – he cites Marx's phrase 'ignorant perfection'. Howe counters that they are indeed plebeian, but that this has little to do with being educationally deprived and a good deal more to do with religion. (Though the quarrel between the two critics here is based primarily on the novels, it does have some bearing on our interpretation of *Ivan Denisovich*.):

> The plebeian stress in Tolstoy and Dostoevsky, which one
> hears again in Solzhenitsyn, draws upon a strand of Christian
> belief very powerful in Russian culture, a strand that favors
> egalitarianism and ascetic humility, as if to take the word of
> Jesus at face value. Platon Karataev may himself be an
> example of 'ignorant perfection', but Tolstoy's act in creat-
> ing him is anything but that. [...] And the same might hold
> in regard to Solzhenitsyn's 'plebeian' sentiments.[16]

In this difference of opinion there was at least some sound argumentation.
As more of Solzhenitsyn's works were published in the West, all sorts of
interest groups seized on him for their own ends. Standing midway between
well-considered argument and political hijacking was, for example, Robin
Blackburn's article for *New Left Review*. Concerned primarily with *The First
Circle*, which the critic calls Solzhenitsyn's masterpiece (*Cancer Ward* being
in his view 'weaker'), the piece rates *Ivan Denisovich* 'more modest but entirely
successful', and informs us that 'Above all Solzhenitsyn's work must be read
politically.'[17] It concludes that 'The sentimental moralism of Tolstoy's aristocrat
is simply out of the question for those who have passed through the grinding
ordeal of the labour camps. They do not affect to despise the material bases
of life since they know how degrading [sic. no comma, R.P.] extreme and
prolonged deprivation of them can be. At the same time they are quite beyond
the empty consumerism of the West. In short they still want justice – above all
else – but they never suppose that it is separable from food and drink'.[18]

At the really ludicrous end of politically inspired commentary, the following
two instances are of particular entertainment value: i) *The Workers' Press*,
which its own logo proclaims is 'The daily paper that leads the fight against the
Tory government' and was the organ of the 'Socialist Labour League', a
Trotskyist splinter group, ran a series of lengthy articles on Solzhenitsyn
(February 25, 26, 27 and March 1 and 4 , 1971) by Thomas Jackson, in which
we read, for example, that Solzhenitsyn 'stands four square in defence of the
property values of October', and that Nerzhin, the hero of *The First Circle* was
seeking the Trotskyist path. ii) Some six-seven years later, with the author now
exiled to the West and regularly lambasting the West for its weakness in the
face of communism, we had the British Tory Party repeatedly invoking his
name, usually in garbled form, in its electioneering.[19]

Robin Blackburn may have a point that Solzhenitsyn must be read
politically, but the same could be said of nearly all the great Russian writers.
This notion came out in an engrossing exchange between two heavy-weight
scholars of Russian literature, Max Hayward and Victor Erlich, when they
addressed the early works of Solzhenitsyn. How comforting it is to see that
their respective positions, based on a close reading of just a few works, have
stood the test of time far better than the politically inspired exegeses of a far
larger body of material.

Erlich says of *Ivan Denisovich*:

> The unspeakable squalor and misery, the back-breaking
> labor, and the animal scrounging for scraps of food, is
> authenticated here by a wealth of detail and made more
> credible by the author's quiet, undramatic manner. *One Day*
> is not a horror story. Physical violence appears in the novel
> not as the central actuality but as an ever-present threat [...]
> One cannot but wonder about the cumulative impact of this
> meticulously honest reportage in which thousands of Soviet
> citizens as innocent as Ivan Denisovich, as admirable as the
> brave naval officer Buynovsky, and as appealing as the
> gentle, devout Baptist Aleshka, are doomed to years of
> subhuman existence.

> This is not to say, however, that *One Day* is an overt
> indictment of the system or that, as some over-enthusiastic
> Western exegetes have argued, it implies the notion of the
> forced labor camp as a microcosm of Soviet society. For one
> thing, no work of fiction which could be legitimately inter-
> preted thus would ever secure Khrushchev's personal
> authorization. [...] Though technically *One Day* is a third-
> person narrative, the point of view is provided here by a
> 'simple' peasant, whose potential for survival is consider-
> ably greater than his ratiocinative powers.[20]

Erlich then goes on to a discussion of the style of the work, which in his
view is 'a far cry from the colorless, puritan prose of socialist-realist fiction';
but he has reservations: 'The sustained "folksy" stylization which lends
solidarity and color to the verbal texture of *One Day* limits the novel's scope
and import', and he finds some of the praise that has been heaped on the
book in the West to be exaggerated,[21] citing in particular F.D. Reeve's
assertion that *Ivan Denisovich* is 'one of the greatest works of twentieth-
century European fiction'.

Hayward responded in the same issue.[22] He endorsed Erlich's plea that
there should be a 'viable balance between literary and political considerations' in assessing Soviet works of literature. He also makes the general
point that it is impossible to separate politics and literature in the Soviet
context. He disagrees with Erlich on the question of the literary worth of
contemporary Soviet literature, saying that there are 'no recognised standards
for the measurement and comparison of aesthetic values';[23] for the time
being we can only measure them, in Hayward's view, by 'the impact they
have on ourselves', and 'this is all highly personal'.

Specifically, Hayward disagrees with Erlich over *Ivan Denisovich* on two
counts. Firstly, for Hayward the camp does indeed represent a microcosm

of the Soviet Union, and he quotes the passage concerning the harsher
construction site (*Sotsgorodok*), which Ivan is so keen to avoid. On this site
the prisoners must first erect posts and surround themselves with barbed
wire: 'No Soviet reader would miss this ironic suggestion that in the
enforced "building of socialism" the people were in fact building their own
prison. There are other equally explicit passages suggesting that there was
no essential difference between life in the camp and life outside.'[24] At the
end of his article Hayward takes his argument even further: 'It seems to me
that the concentration camp is to be seen not just as a microcosm of life in
the Soviet Union but of life everywhere. The majority of the human race are
condemned to a daily grind, a rat-race of which the concentration camp is
the ultimate and most intense expression.'[25]

   This universality is achieved, in Hayward's analysis, by the very device
that Erlich found so constricting, namely the narrative style of the work.
Solzhenitsyn was anxious that we should see the 'whole experience' not
through the eyes of an intellectual. The hero 'belongs to a totally different
world from that of the intellectuals who can still derive some solace from
conversation, from the feeling of still belonging to a larger intellectual world
outside'. Hayward cites in support of this the passage where Ivan notes
mentally that Muscovites can smell each other out and chatter away among
themselves so that for him they might just as well be speaking in Latvian or
Rumanian. Hayward concludes:

> Solzhenitsyn has achieved something which many Russian
> authors in the past have striven for but never quite managed.
> Tolstoy's attempts to depict 'simple people' are not entirely
> successful. His muzhiks are too obviously intended to dem-
> onstrate some 'truth', arrived at by Tolstoy in the course of
> his intellectual quest, to be convincing in their own right.
> To take another 'classical' example, Sholokhov's Grigorii
> Melekhov is suspect as a genuinely 'popular' type. He has
> all the external attributes of a Cossack, but one cannot help
> feeling that his attitudes, his responses to life are somehow
> 'intellectualised'. His inner doubts, his 'Hamletism,' the
> 'romantic' flavor of his love for Aksinia – all this vaguely
> echoes literary models and leaves me at least with the
> suspicion that Sholokhov has introduced us to the workings
> of his own comparatively sophisticated mind rather than to
> a completely non-intellectual, even if highly intelligent,
> Cossack. Isaac Babel's Cossacks, by contrast, are far more
> convincing because they are observed only *externally* –
> Babel was aware of the dangers of the intellectual trying 'to
> get under the skin' of the 'simple man' and did not even
> attempt it. I am inclined to believe that Solzhenitsyn has

come nearest to achieving this almost, by its very nature, impossible task. One feature of Stalin's concentration camps was that for the first time the intelligentsia really got to know the *narod*; and *One Day* is an attempt to transmute this knowledge, obtained in such tragic circumstances, into a work of literature.[26]

Hayward does not accept Erlich's opinion that Khrushchev would hardly permit the publication of a thorough-going indictment of the Soviet system, arguing that the Soviet leader was more than capable of embarking on schemes which misfired. Hayward's purely literary perceptions, quoted at length above, are worthy of the most serious consideration. Of particular note is his notion that *Ivan Denisovich* is applicable in ways far broader than its immediate geographical-temporal setting suggests. Elsewhere, Hayward returns to the same theme:

> One day in the life of Ivan Denisovich seems uncannily symbolic of one day in *anybody's* life. Like Kafka's *The Trial*, Solzhenitsyn's novel shows the human condition as a captive state from which there is no escape and for which there is no rational explanation. The feeling of being trapped and doomed is considerably heightened by making the reader see the concentration camp through the eyes of an illiterate peasant who is unable to rationalise his predicament as an intellectual would.[27]

Hayward refers to the adapted form of *skaz* that the author uses, and in another article again raises the issue of *Ivan Denisovich* having more universal appeal than a first reading might suggest: in a wide-ranging survey 'Themes and Variations in Soviet Literature, 1917-1967' he identified an exact parallel between the image of the prisoners in *Ivan Denisovich* building their own compound with the same metaphor in The Epilogue to *Doctor Zhivago*, where one of the hero's friends who survived the purges describes how they, as prisoners, were brought to an open field in a forest: 'We cut down the wood to build our own dungeons, we surrounded ourselves with a stockade, we equipped ourselves with prison-cells and watch-towers'.[28] In 'The Decline of Socialist Realism' he states again, with specific reference to *Ivan Denisovich*, that the building of socialism in Russia is expressly likened to the setting up of a concentration camp.[29]

The politics, the message, the style, the characters, the plot of *Ivan Denisovich* all figure in the views we have alluded to so far. However, does the book possess some definable 'philosophy', a *mirovozzrenie* (world outlook)? Hayward certainly hints at one, but it was left to Geoffrey Hosking to expatiate on the matter, and it is significant that he does so by coupling his interpretation of the work with *Doctor Zhivago*. He points out that Pasternak and Solzhenitsyn stood out from so many other writers of the Thaw period because they 'rediscovered philosophy and folk culture'.[30] The philosophy which many of the post-Stalin authors found so attractive was, according to Hosking, that of the *Landmarks* (*Vekhi*) group and before them, Dostoevsky. These intellectuals – Russian intellectuals – rejected Marxism and they attached importance to spirit and individual personality, rather than to social groups, classes. They were suspicious of causality in man's behaviour, and they were attracted to the Russian Orthodox Church. Such profound considerations are not immediately apparent in *Ivan Denisovich*; and one must guard against reading into the text all the aspects of Solzhenitsyn's life and thought which he was later to develop at great length in his publicistic works as well as in his creative writing.

We can, however, isolate one aspect of his philosophy, implicit in Hosking's analysis, namely, the existentialist preoccupation with the here and now as opposed to some teleological contemplation of a bright future. This outlook is summed up in Yuri Zhivago's over-quoted words: 'Man is born to live, not to prepare for life.' Ivan Denisovich Shukhov is, in the view of the present critic, the living embodiment of this dictum. As such, he doubtlessly owes something to anti-Marxist Russian philosophy, but he also – perhaps inadvertently as far as his creator is concerned – owes something to Camus' *The Myth of Sisyphus*.

There are many commentaries in books and journals on *Ivan Denisovich* and most of them have a lot to recommend them. The ones that have been mentioned here more or less define the parameters of all the various discussions that the book has spawned. Our own close reading of the text is not likely to go much *beyond* what has already been said, but it will have its own special emphases and will, at times, take issue with the individual interpretations put forward by other critics.

Notes to Part One

Introduction (pp. 3-17)

1. Labedz, L., *Solzhenitsyn: A Documentary Record*, (Second Edition), Harmondsworth, 1974, p. 58 and p. 50.

2. Dunlop, J., Haugh, R., Nicholson, M. (eds.) *Solzhenitsyn in Exile: Critical Essays and Documentary Materials*, Stanford, 1985, p. 119.

3. Solzhenitsyn, A. *Bodalsyia telёnok s dubom*, p. 462.

4. In Erofeyev, V. and Reynolds, A. (eds.) *The Penguin Book of New Russian Writing*, Harmondsworth, 1995, p. 348. This story translated by Andrew Bromfield.

5. Johnson, P., *Khrushchev and The Arts*, Cambridge, Massachusetts, 1965, p. 103.

6. Hingley,R., *Russian Writers and Soviet Society*, London, 1979, p. 16.

7. Chukhontsev, O. (ed.), *Dissonant Voices: The New Russian Fiction*, Harvill, London, 1991, p. 89. This story translated by Michael Duncan.

8. Khrushchev, N., *Khrushchev Remembers*, translated by Strobe Talbot, London, 1971, p. 252.

9. Khrushchev, N., *Khrushchev Remembers: The Glasnost Tapes*, translated and edited by Jerrold Schector with Vyacheslav Luchkov, London, 1990, p. 196.

10. See Solzhenitsyn's Note to the Paris-Vermont 1973 edition (authorised version). Michael Scammell, working from the transcript of an interview, in which Solzhenitsyn was recalling presumably somewhat casually and at speed, says it was 1952. (Scammell, M., *Solzhenitsyn: A Biography*, New York, 1984, London, 1985, p. 382.

11. *The Gulag Archipelago*, vol. 3, translated by Harry Willetts, London, 1976, p. 275 and p. 279. For the corresponding passage in the Russian original see *Sobranie sochinenii*, YMCA Press, Paris-Vermont, 1978, vol. 7, p. 276 and pp. 280-1.

12. Frankel, E., *Novy Mir: A Case Study in the Politics of Literature 1952-1958*, Cambridge, 1981, pp. 17-19.

13. *Cancer Ward*, Part II, translated by Nicholas Bethell and David Burg, London, 1969, pp. 23-8. For the corresponding passage in the Russian original see *Sobranie sochinenii*, vol. 4, pp. 298-303.

14. *Cancer Ward*, Part 1, translated as above, London, 1968, p. 52. For the corresponding passage in the Russian original see *Sobranie sochinenii*, vol. 4, p. 48.

15. *Cancer Ward*, Part 1, pp. 326-338. For the corresponding Russian original see *Sobranie sochinenii*, vol. 4, pp. 271-80.

16. Kazak, V., *Entsiklopedicheskii slovar' russkoi literatury s 1917 goda*, London, 1988, p. 749.

17. Swayze, H., *Political Control of Literature in the USSR, 1946-1959*, Cambridge, Massachusetts, 1962, pp. 248-9.

18. Scammell, p. 354.

19. Of the several versions of the work see for example *V kruge pervom*, Paris, 1969, p. 418 and *V pervom krugu*, London, 1968, p. 402. Interestingly, this passage is omitted from the Collected Works (see *Sobranie sochinenii*, vol. 2, pp. 96-7), presumably because the author, by now regarded as a great writer in the West, wished to guard against accusations of arrogance.

20. *Bodalsia*, p. 23.

21. Kaiser, R., 'Afterword' in L. Kopelev, *No Jail for Thought*, translated by Anthony Austin, London, 1977, p. 263.

22. Scammell, p. 408.

23. See Reshetovskaia, *Aleksandr Solzhenitsyn i chitaiushchaia Rossiia*, Sovetskaia Rossiia, Moscow, 1990, p. 52, where Reshetovskaia, Solzhenitsyn's first wife, reports Kopelev's reaction. Solzhenitsyn himself, in an expanded edition of *Bodalsia* also reports that Kopelev regarded *Ivan Denisovich* as a 'production story' (*proizvodstvennaia povest'*), adding that Kopelev's wife handed over the manuscript to Berzer somewhat casually, without any particular instructions (See *Bodalsia telënok s dubom*, Soglasie, Moscow, 1996, pp. 522-523). This rather contradicts Scammell's account. See below.

24. Scammell, p. 413.

25. *Bodalsia*, p. 86.

26. It is worth noting Lakshin's reaction when he first read the work. He recalls that Tvardovsky gave him the manuscript to read in early December 1961, telling him not to say a word to anyone and to return it in a day or two. He read it through without a break, handing the pages over to his wife, so she could read it in tandem. 'There was originality, and power, and truth! We fell asleep, I think, about 4 o'clock in the morning.' Lakshin, V., *Novyi mir vo vremena Khrushchëva*, Knizhnaia palata, Moscow, 1991, p. 50.

27. Ellis, F., *Vasiliy Grossman: The Genesis and Evolution of a Russian Heretic*, Oxford, 1994, pp. 11-15.

28. Scammell, p. 430. Lakshin and Reshetovskaia have also provided accounts of this meeting, in the former's case, at first hand. See Lakshin, V., *Novyi mir vo vremena Khrushchëva*, Knizhnaia palata, Moscow, 1991, pp. 66-67 and Reshetovskaia, N., *Aleksandr Solzhenitsyn i chitaiushchaia Rossiia*, pp. 62-63.

29. Lakshin, p. 73.

30. Scammell, p. 434.

Chapter I (pp. 18-28)

1. See Busch, R., 'Gladkov's *Cement*: The Making of a Soviet Classic', *Slavic and East European Journal*, no. 22, 1978, pp. 348-361. For a highly detailed examination of the various changes in Gladkov's text, which argues, daringly for its time, that not all of them were for the best, see L. Smirnova, 'Kak sozdavalsia "Tsement"' in *Tekstologiia proizvedenii sovetskoi literatury*, Nauka, Akademiia nauk, Moscow, 1967, pp. 140-227.

2. Scammell, pp. 901-2; and 'D', *Stremia 'Tikhogo Dona' (zagadki romana)*, Paris, 1974, *Predislovie* A. Solzhenitsyn. The anonymous author 'D' was in fact Irina Medvedeva-Tomashevskaya.

3. Kern, G., 'Solženicyn's Self-Censorship: The Canonical text of *Odin den' Ivana Denisoviča*', *Slavic and East European Journal*, Vol. 20, no. 4, 1976, pp. 421-436, p. 426.

4. *Bodalsia*, p. 46. Lakshin (pp. 66-67) also offers an account of this 'difficult' meeting on 23 July 1962. This was the first time he had met Solzhenitsyn. To objections that Solzhenitsyn makes Buynovsky turn from being a thinking, feeling human being into a dumb animal, the author retorted that he himself had had to do the same or he would probably have perished.

5. Scammell, p. 439.

6. Kern, p. 430.

7. *Bodalsia*, p. 19.

Chapter II

Responses in the Soviet Union (pp. 29-40)

1. Tvardovsky, A., 'Vmesto predisloviia', *Novyi mir*, no. 11, 1962, pp. 8-9, p. 8. The translation here, as elsewhere, is fairly literal and seeks to convey the wordiness of Soviet literary criticism.

2. Lakshin, V., *Solzhenitsyn, Tvardovsky and* Novy mir, translated and edited by Michael Glenny, Cambridge, Massachusetts, 1980, p. 5.

3. Quoted in Nicholson, M., *Aleksandr Solzhenitsyn and the Russian Literary Tradition*, unpublished doctorate, University of Oxford, 1974, p. 146. This work has many sterling qualities, most germanely here, a very thorough survey of Soviet responses to *Ivan Denisovich* and other works.

4. Lakshin, V., 'Ivan Denisovich, ego druz'ia i nedrugi', *Novyi mir*, no. 1, 1964, pp. 223-245. This article was reprinted in *Sobranie sochinenii*, Possev, Frankfurt, 1969-1970, vol. 6, pp. 243-286. See also in this volume a fuller account of Solzhenitsyn's Soviet reception: Tarasova, N., 'Vkhozhdenie Solzhenitsyna v sovetskuiu literaturu i diskussii o nëm', pp. 197-242.

5. Lakshin, p. 223.

6. Lakshin, p. 224.

7. Lakshin, p. 225.

8. Lakshin, p. 226.

9. Lakshin, p. 227.

10. Lakshin, p. 227.

11. Lakshin, p. 229.

12. Lakshin, p. 230.

13. Lakshin, p. 231.

14. Lakshin, p. 233.

15. Lakshin, p. 236.

16. Lakshin, p. 239.

17. Lakshin, pp. 243-4.

18. Lakshin, p. 245.

19. Vinokur, T., 'O iazyke i stile povesti A. I. Solzhenitsyna "Odin den' Ivana Denisovicha"', *Voprosy kul'tury rechi*, 1965, no. 6, pp. 16-32.

20. Vinokur, pp. 16-17.

21. Vinokur, p. 21.

22. Vinokur, p. 19.

23. Pascal, R., *The Dual Voice*, Manchester University Press, 1977, p. 26.

24. Vinokur, p. 26.

25. Vinokur, p. 25.

26. Vinokur, p. 32.

Critical Responses in the West (pp. 40-49)

1. Zekulin, G., 'Solzhenitsyn's Four Stories', *Soviet Studies*, vol. XVI, no. 1, 1964, pp. 45-62.

2. Zekulin, p. 45.

3. Zekulin, p. 46.

4. Zekulin, p. 47.

5. Zekulin, p. 48.

6. Zekulin, p. 61.

7. Lukács, G., *Solzhenitsyn*, translated from the German by William Graf, London, 1969, p. 7.

8. Lukács, p. 10.

9. Lukács, p. 12.

10. Lukács, p. 13.

11. Lukács, p. 16.

12. Lukács, p. 19.

13. Lukács, p. 20.

14. Lukács, p. 33.

15. Howe, I., 'Lukacs and Solzhenitsyn' in Dunlop, J. et al (eds.), *Aleksandr Solzhenitsyn: Critical Essays and Documentary Materials*, Hoover Press Publications, Stanford, 1985, pp. 147-155, p. 151.

16. Howe, p. 154.

17. Blackburn, R., 'The First Circle', *New Left Review*, Sept/Oct., 1970, pp. 56-64, p. 56.

18. Blackburn, p. 64.

19. The writer, critic and satirist, Clive James, had great fun at Margaret Thatcher's expense over this. See 'Case of Torynitskyn', *Observer*, April 9, 1978, p. 35.

20. Erlich, V., 'Post-Stalin Trends in Russian Literature', *Slavic Review*, no. 3, 1964, pp. 405-419, pp. 409-10.

21. Erlich, p. 411.

22. Hayward, M., 'Solzhenitsyn's Place in Contemporary Soviet Literature', *Slavic Review*, no. 3, 1964, pp. 432-436.

23. Hayward, p. 433.

24. Hayward, pp. 434-5.

25. Hayward, p. 436.

26. Hayward, pp. 435-6.

27. Hayward, M., *Writers in Russia 1917-1978*, edited and with an Introduction by Patricia Blake, London, 1983, pp. 72-3.

28. Ibid. , pp. 142-3.

29. Ibid., pp. 173-4.

30. Hosking, G., *Beyond Socialist Realism: Soviet Fiction since* Ivan Denisovich, London and New York, 1980, p. 32.

Part Two

The following three chapters will seek to follow up some of the purely literary remarks that other commentators have made, the references to Tolstoy, Dostoevsky, epic, realism, truth, Solzhenitsyn's descriptive powers and so on. We shall start with the contention of Max Hayward that there is in *Ivan Denisovich* a Kafka connection, since on the surface this seems a trifle outlandish.

I.   A Modernist Text?

Solzhenitsyn's dissatisfaction with what can be called broadly 'Modernism' is well attested. In Volume II of *The Gulag Achipelago* he describes the harrowing conditions of one of his own periods of forced labour (hewing clay with his bare hands in the dead of night, the rain falling) and adds:

> Somewhere young men of our age were studying at the Sorbonne or at Oxford, playing tennis during their ample hours of relaxation, arguing about the problems of the world in student cafés. They were already being published and were exhibiting their paintings. They were twisting and turning to find ways of distorting the insufficiently original world around them in some new way. They railed against the classics for exhausting all the subjects and themes. They railed at their own governments and their own reactionaries who did not want to comprehend and adopt the advanced experience of the Soviet Union.[1]

Here one detects, of course, that Solzhenitsyn's real disdain is for Western artists of left-wing persuasion who see art as being something other than purely representational. It was certainly the case that, for example, surrealism (just one of many artistic movements in the early part of the twentieth century to come under the general umbrella of 'Modernism'), especially in the manner in which it originated in France during the inter-war years, was closely associated with the revolutionary left. Paul Éluard was fêted in the capitals of Eastern Europe in the post-war years, just at the time when Solzhenitsyn was a slave labourer. Moreover, Solzhenitsyn's distrust of Modernist trends in literature was compounded by ignorance – Kafka, Joyce, Proust and others received at best only token, and highly selective, publication in the Soviet Union even when Solzhenitsyn was at liberty.

His refusal to meet Sartre and Simone de Beauvoir when they were on a visit to Moscow in the spring of 1966 gives some ground for further speculation. As a newly 'discovered' author, perhaps he was shy, or possibly too proud at the prospect of meeting arguably the world's most famous living writer and philosopher. Solzhenitsyn himself has gone on record that he was loath to meet Sartre because the latter had championed Sholokhov, that stalwart of the Soviet establishment, for the Nobel Prize, and that the meeting might strengthen Sartre's reputation for broadmindedness while doing nothing for Solzhenitsyn.[2] Whatever the case, given Solzhenitsyn's increasing insistence on traditional concepts like 'conscience' and 'truth', it is difficult to see how he could cope with Sartre's more abstract cast of mind, his formulation of 'mauvaise foi' and, most decisively, his sporadic support for the Soviet government and, later on, for Maoism.

The vast bulk of what Solzhenitsyn has written could be broadly classified as 'realism': flesh-and-blood characters, historical accuracy, vivid and precise descriptions of places and things. But he would not be unaware of Modernism as it had manifested itself in Russia before the First World War and as it had struggled for survival in the 1920s before being extinguished by Socialism Realism, with some of its leading exponents executed or driven to suicide, emigration, prison or silence. There is one obvious instance in Solzhenitsyn's *oeuvre* where he does adopt a more experimental method. *The Red Wheel* incorporates snatches from the news media of the day to highlight historical events as they unfold, and critics were also quick to see the 'film scenario' sections in the work as a technique owing something to Dos Passos. A supreme irony of Solzhenitsyn's life story is to be found in the fact that he was able to read at least some of the banned 'modernist' writers when he was in prison in the Lubyanka in Moscow – Zamyatin, Pilnyak, Merezhkovsky – and the American, Dos Passos.

All we are saying here is that Solzhenitsyn's animus against Modernism is not wholesale. If we attempt a working definition of the term, we can see how, in fact, it might hold some appeal for him. For most critics Modernism began around 1890 and lasted beyond the Second World War; it may still be with us and/or it may have shaded into Post-Modernism. It is also generally agreed that its high point was the first quarter of this century and relates especially to Yeats, Joyce, Eliot, Lawrence as far as English literature is concerned and to Proust, Valéry, Gide, Mann, Rilke and Kafka as regards Continental literatures.[3] In their examination Bradbury and McFarlane, while repeatedly allowing for the difficulties over dating and definition, write:

> The movement towards sophistication and mannerism, towards introversion, technical display, internal self-deception, has often been taken as a common base for a *definition* of Modernism. Certainly, a number of technical features do reappear from movement to movement, even when these are radically at odds in other ways: anti-representationalism in painting, atonalism in music, *vers libre* in poetry, stream-of-consciousness narrative in the novel.[4]

They refer to Frank Kermode's observation to the effect that Modernism involves a tendency to bring form closer to chaos, thus producing a sense of 'formal desperation', and they continue:

This, in turn, suggests that Modernism might mean not only a new mode or mannerism in the arts, but a certain magnificent disaster for them. In short, experimentalism does not simply suggest the presence of sophistication, difficulty and novelty in art; it also suggests bleakness, darkness, alienation, disintegration [...] The crisis is a crisis of culture; it often involves an unhappy view of history – so that the Modernist writer is not simply the artist set free, but the artist under specific, apparently historical strain.[5]

Of course, Modernism was born well before the First World War, but the trauma wrought between 1914 and 1918 (and for the Russians a good way beyond) vindicated the Modernist view of the world and gave it fresh impetus. Again Bradbury and McFarlane:

Modernism [...] is the art consequent on Heisenberg's 'Uncertainty Principle', of the destruction of civilisation and reason in the First World War, of the world changed and reinterpreted by Marx, Freud and Darwin, of capitalism and constant industrial acceleration, of existential exposure to meaninglessness or absurdity. It is the literature of technology. It is the art consequent on the dis-establishing of communal reality and conventional notions of causality, on the destruction of traditional notions of the wholeness of individual character, on the linguistic chaos that ensues when public notions of language have been discredited and when all realities have become subjective fictions.[6]

It is a safe bet that Solzhenitsyn would not have much time for some of the wordiness here; but he would acknowledge the historical circumstances identified in Bradbury's and McFarlane's analysis and would argue that Russians have been even more the victims of the new world order that was born out of the First World War than have Westerners. Hence his primary allegiance to 'realism' in his attempt to convey that experience to a wider world. Yet there are many features of *Ivan Denisovich* which a Western reader could readily relate to the foregoing comments on Modernism. That, for a Western reader, Solzhenitsyn's text can be understood in Modernist terms may also be due in part to a 'perception-gap'. Allowing for the fact that a Westerner's historical and social experience – in most instances more settled and comfortable – is different from a Russian's, the Western reader has a built-in tendency to interpret metaphorically what to a Russian is straightforward realistic description. The Czech novelist, Josef Škvorecký, has a tragi-comic episode in his novel *The Engineer of Human Souls* in which the hero's Canadian students have just seen a film about a prominent victim of the 1950s show trials in Czechoslovakia. When he tells them that he knew personally the victim's wife, his students, unable to contemplate that there was a real man behind the part played by an actor, ask if she too was in films! In short, for a Western reader's *aesthetic* experience, it is irrelevant whether Ivan Denisovich was based on a real man or whether, like Kafka's heroes, he grew out of a troubled imagination. However, for any reader, Western or otherwise, to be moved in terms of political, social and even moral outlook, it is of crucial importance that Solzhenitsyn's story be grounded in 'real life'.

There are two obvious nodal points in our devil's advocacy: Kafka's *The Trial* (begun in 1914, published 1925) and Joyce's *Ulysses* (written 1913-20, full text published 1922).

Kafka's novel – like his story *Metamorphosis* (written 1912, published 1915) and like *Ivan Denisovich* – opens at the start of the day, and one might say that each of these stories represents an inversion of conventional realism, for in each one the hero (and the reader) awakes into a nightmare. A common, but to many sophisticates, a crude, interpretation of *The Trial* is that it is a prophecy of the totalitarianism, fascist or communist, which was to engulf much of Europe. Crude it may be, but how could the opening of the work *fail* to apply to Ivan Denisovich and to so many of the other guiltless prisoners that populate Solzhenitsyn's books:

> Someone must have been telling lies about Joseph K., for without having done anything wrong he was arrested one fine morning. His landlady's cook, who always brought him his breakfast at eight o'clock, failed to appear on this occasion. That had never happened before. K. waited for a little while longer, watching from his pillow the old lady opposite, who seemed to be peering at him with a curiosity unusual even for her, but then, feeling both put out and hungry, he rang the bell. At once there was a knock at the door and a man entered whom he had never seen before in the house.[7]

Yet if the surface facts here run parallel to Ivan's biography (the motiveless arrest of an innocent man) the underlying manner of the narrative is also close to that of *Ivan Denisovich*. Kafka's prose draws its strength from the mundane recounting of highly improbable or sometimes utterly fantastic events. As Erich Heller puts it: 'Kafka's style, simple lucid and "real" in the sense of never leaving any doubt concerning the reality – in contrast to any artificial or contrived quality – of that which is narrated, described or meditated, does yet narrate, describe or meditate the shockingly unbelievable.' The result is, in Heller's view, that the reader is forced to ask, in vain, what it all means, yet 'the narrated event [...] defies any established intellectual order and familiar form of understanding, and thus arouses the kind of intellectual anxiety that greedily and compulsively reaches out for interpretations'.[8]

Everything in Ivan's world has a meaning and a reason, at least to the extent that the hero remains throughout unpuzzled, unquestioning and, unlike the reader, unappalled. Soviet readers pounced on explanations, political and moral, for Ivan's predicament. Yet, as we have noted already, Solzhenitsyn was adamant that his hero should be a thoroughly uncerebral type. We recall also that in the first draft of the work there was no reference at all to Stalin (i.e. no reference to the most obvious cause of the prisoners' sorry lot), thus reinforcing this 'uncertainty principle'. While in the first few short paragraphs of the book, the reader's bewilderment grows (are we in an army barracks? no, given that the man beating reveille is a *nadziratel'*, not someone with a military rank, and what are a *zona* and a *parasha*?), Ivan is introduced as a thoroughly sensible and self-possessed individual who can marshal his precious free time to good effect: 'anyone who knows camp life can always earn a bit on the side', and we are promptly given several examples of how.[9]

There are frequent examples of the abnormal, slightly fantastic world which Ivan inhabits and the matter-of-fact way he reacts to it. He utters scarcely a word of protest when the Tartar guard leads him away for punishment because he has overslept (so unjust given that Ivan is a regular early-riser and today is feeling ill) (Paris, p.10; Willetts, p. 5). Immediately following this we have the stark description of the scene outside the barracks hut: 'Two large search lights were criss-crossing the compound from the distant corner towers. The lights in the compound and the interior lights were shining. There were so many of them dotted around that they completely outshone the stars' (Paris, p.11; Willetts, p. 6); and the same image is picked up on a few pages later: 'It was still just as dark in that sky, from which the camp lights had chased the stars' (Paris, p.16; Willetts, p. 13). Man's artefacts here have – at least momentarily – defeated and negated the natural order. One should note here that the scene is described in the relatively neutral voice of the narrator, not as Ivan's thought processes and in his vernacular; and that no explanation is offered. Thus the reader is as disarmed and numbed as is the hero when faced with abomination.

In the few instances when Ivan is not governed by common sense and the urge to survive, his actions, like those of many other prisoners, spring from a stated sense of decorum, linked closely with personal dignity. The prisoners in the mess hall consider it bad manners to spit the fish bones directly on to the floor – they are spat out on the table and then the pile is swept on to the floor before the next gang arrives. No matter how cold he is, Ivan always removes his headgear when eating indoors.

By contrast, the real reasons behind the actions of the overseers and indeed the very *raison d'être* of the camp are never explored. The order created by officialdom seems to consist almost entirely of absurdities. Ivan may not know it, but the *fel'dsher* in the sick-bay has no medical training. He is a student of literature, whom the doctor has taken on so that he can write the poems that he was forbidden to write when a free man (Paris, p. 20;

Willetts, p. 17). Irrespective of whether one is ill or not there is a strict quota of just two prisoners who can be excused work on health grounds in the mornings. The brutal disciplinary officer with the apt name of Volkovoi (deriving from the word for 'wolf') once used to carry a whip and use it to bloody effect on the prisoners; but we are informed in a one-sentence paragraph that 'Now for some reason he had stopped carrying the whip' (Paris, p. 26; Willetts, p. 26). The reader might waste time speculating as to why (have Volkovoi's superiors intervened, has he had qualms of conscience, has he become afraid of his charges? Certainly the mood in the camp is changing and stool pigeons are being murdered, as we learn elsewhere (Paris, p. 50, Willetts p. 58). As we noted in Chapter One, in *The Gulag Archipelago* Solzhenitsyn argues that at the beginning of the 1950s the camp system was indeed facing mutiny). Yet illogicality and absurdity, as much as injustice and cruelty, are really at issue here. A similar device is used in the letter from home that Ivan recalls: his wife talks of imprisonment being the punishment for not fulfilling the work norm on the kolkhoz, but 'for some reason that law was not brought in' (Paris, p. 31; Willetts, p. 33).

Another Kafkaesque dimension to *Ivan Denisovich* concerns the pointlessness and endlessness, at least from the prisoners' point of view, that inform much of the activity. When the prisoners are marched out of the compound they pass a woodworking plant and a residential block and a recreational club, all of which they have built, but which others, free workers, occupy. Then immediately we are given a view of the barren terrain: 'The column marched out on to the steppe straight into the wind and the reddening dawn. The bare white snow lay stretching out from one extremity to the other, both left and right, and there wasn't a single sapling [or possibly 'stunted tree'? – *derevtsa ... ni odnogo*] anywhere on the steppe' (Paris, pp. 30-1; Willetts, p. 32). The very next sentence informs us that a new year has started, that it is 1951. So we have a rapid transition from work from which only others benefit to geographical expanse bereft of life, and on to an allusion to time. In his search for the nature of his guilt Joseph K.'s professional life becomes irrelevant; in *The Castle* the hero, despite his best efforts, cannot take up his appointment as a land-surveyor. There is an unfinished quality to all Kafka's major novels, and as such they exemplify the distrust that Modernist perceptions of the world display towards history. Modern man cannot effectively participate in his own fate or perform a useful role in history; he is simply its victim.

This leads us on to a consideration of the time planes in *Ivan Denisovich*. Firstly, there is the minute-by-minute, hour-by-hour time-frame of which Ivan is persistently aware, despite the absence of clocks and watches – even in the sick-bay, we are told, there is no wall clock; the bosses keep the time for the prisoners (Paris, p.19; Willetts, p.16). Ivan can be intensely conscious of every second, whether it be spent in the savouring of his meagre rations or when he is frenetically engaged in work. Given that the narrative is shot through with reminiscences, reflections, mental observations, dialogues and asides, it may be as well to outline Ivan's movements during his day.

He wakes up in the barracks hut, is led off by the guard to wash the floor in the HQ hut; then he goes to the mess hall for breakfast, then on to the sick bay, then back to his hut. He goes outside with the rest of his work brigade, has his serial numbers touched up by one of the camp 'artists'; after that comes the search at the camp gates; outside the camp, the prisoners are marched in a column to the building site, which is surrounded by watch towers and a fence; Ivan's brigade takes shelter in a car repair shed, while the bosses are deciding where they are to work that day; they are assigned to the brick-laying on the power station; Ivan and Kildigs filch a roll of tarred paper from another part of the site to block the window openings in the building where they are working, so as to keep some heat in; having arranged everything for the bricklaying to begin, they go over to the on-site mess hut for dinner; Ivan takes a bowl of gruel over to the trusty Tsezar in the site manager's office; after the extended bricklaying episode, which builds to a crescendo of activity for the hero and his immediate associates, there is the delay at the site gates while the prisoners are counted and recounted; then follows the march, which turns into a race with the column of engineers, back to the camp; then comes the search at the gates, before Ivan goes to the post room to save a place in the queue for Tsezar who is to collect a parcel; next he returns to his hut to pick up the bread he saved from the morning and then he makes for the mess hall; after supper he goes over to hut 7 and buys tobacco from the Latvian; when he is back in his own hut, we hear the captain's story about the Americans in Sevastopol being duped; after two roll calls where the prisoners are taken out of the hut, Ivan finally settles down in his bunk.

The other time plane involves Ivan's relationship to history. He has been in prison for eight years; he has not seen his wife since June 23, 1941; one of his dearest possessions is the spoon he fashioned himself and which is etched with the words 'Ust'-Izhma, 1944', referring to the previous camp he was in. He has less than two years to serve, but is only too aware that prisoners are often given a second term (Paris, pp. 48-9; Willetts, p.56). He recalls his pre-war rural life and his war experiences. The closing words of the story – set out as a separate section consisting of two brief paragraphs – have acquired the status of holy writ in the canon of Russian literature:

> In his sentence from bell to bell there were three thousand six hundred and fifty-three such days.

> Because of the leap years there were three days extra added on. (Paris, p.120; Willetts, p. 150)

One needs to note that if Kafka's works remain 'incomplete' in some way, the very opposite is true of Solzhenitsyn's. One recalls, in addition to the quotation above, in particular the resonant endings to *Matryona's Home*, *Cancer Ward*, and *The First Circle*. In these last three works there is an element of overt moralising, but in *Ivan Denisovich* the tone is more restrained and more ambivalent. On the one hand the closing words reflect the author's persistent urge to *engage* history: put simplistically, to set the historical record straight (a passion most clearly on display in *The Red Wheel* and *The Gulag Archipelago*). On the other hand, they underscore with mild irony Ivan's inability even to comprehend, let alone to help shape, historical events. His own biography is all that counts, and, given his current predicament, only on a day-to-day basis. This notion is ultimately far more subversive to Marxism-Leninism than any routine exposé of Stalin's crimes. It also links in with our second nodal point.

Ulysses is a mock epic which takes place in one day. Joyce's stated mission as a writer was to divorce art and life, to make language the reality. Solzhenitsyn's artistic impetus could hardly be further from Joyce's, and it is certainly the case that he employs an adapted form of *skaz*, a 'dual voice', rather than Joyce's 'stream of consciousness', whereby the individual's thought processes are communicated to the reader, apparently without the ordering function of the intermediary, the writer. Yet are the results so very different for the reader, bombarded as he/she is with a range of immediate mental processes and responses, verbalised or otherwise? Moreover, Joyce creates a world in which drama and epic are certainly possible within the confines of a single day, since, for him, the real world resides primarily within the individual human psyche. One might also note the *prima facie* parallel that both Leopold Bloom and Ivan Denisovich emerge 'from home', go out into the world for one day, and then return.

While Solzhenitsyn considers the Russian Revolution to be the great catastrophe of the century, Joyce's attitude to it is studied indifference: Neil Cornwell has recorded that in 1932, in response to a questionnaire concerning his attitude to the October Revolution from a lady called Romanova of 'The International Union of Revolutionary Writers' in Moscow, Joyce merely pointed out that the said Revolution had occurred in November, and that to judge from the signature on the questionnaire 'the changes cannot amount to much'.[10] Solzhenitsyn has created a character who is similarly indifferent, even if he is unable to verbalise his attitudes. Ivan never contemplates the facts of the Revolution, nor its rights and wrongs; and likewise, the war, which has affected him so cruelly, is never a subject for debate for him.

In his discussion of Modernism Alan Bullock illustrates the ambivalence of our century with reference to two pictures:

> One is a photograph of a London street-scene taken in the summer of 1904 [the year that *Ulysses* is set in, as it happens]; it shows the busy crossing in front of the Royal Exchange [...] businessmen in top hats [...] clerks in bowler

hats, a ragged newspaper boy [...] hansom-cabs, brewers' drays, waggons and horse-drawn buses – the animated everyday scene on any day of the week in the largest and wealthiest city in the world, caught suddenly and pinned down in black and white.[11]

Bullock's second image is *Les Demoiselles d'Avignon*, painted by Picasso in 1907, 'a painting fertilized by Spanish and African influence which has been called the first truly twentieth-century painting: five naked women painted in a series of geometrical lozenges and triangles, with total disregard of anatomy and perspective'.[12]

As Bullock reminds us, the turn of the century and its first two decades witnessed an unprecedented acceleration in practically all branches of human endeavour – economics and technology, physics, sociology and psychology. The photograph gives an impression of the 1900s 'of an age remarkably unselfconscious, self-confident, far less troubled by the anxieties, fears and fantasies, the self-consciousness and guilt which may tremble underneath a few of its writings but which have found such vivid expression and subscription in Europe since then'.[13] Picasso's painting, by contrast, is just one example of an extraordinary flowering in nearly all the branches of the arts, visual, musical, literary (which many of the major cities of Europe saw at the same time) which conveys a far more troubled image of modern man. The artists who were attuned to the problems lurking beneath the surface of the scientific and technological advances were in a minority, but their misapprehensions proved to be well-founded.

One might argue that the photograph Bullock cites, with its untroubled self-confidence, once injected with some revolutionary romanticism, was to become pretty much the template for Soviet Socialist Realism, while Picasso's painting and the entire trend which it represented could only be explained away by Soviet cultural experts as bourgeois degeneracy or as the anguished depiction of a doomed capitalist order. Manifestations of degeneracy or doom which applied too obviously to the Soviet system were consequently outlawed. Hence the cloud under which, during the Soviet era, most of the leading Russian Modernist writers (Akhmatova, Bely, Mandelshtam, Pasternak, Pilnyak, Zamyatin and many more) fell.

We selected *The Trial* and *Ulysses* for comparative purposes primarily because they are two of the best known examples of Modernist texts; but being from non-Russian literature they also help to highlight the universality of Solzhenitsyn's work. A point of comparison much closer to home would be Zamyatin's novel *We*, written in 1920, but published in the Soviet Union only in 1988. This work, acknowledged by George Orwell as the inspiration for his *1984* and believed by many also to be at the back of Aldous Huxley's *Brave New World*, has been the subject of endless discussion in terms of the irrational. In some of its minutiae its prophecy, as regards the Soviet Union, has proved chillingly accurate: the characters are all designated by numbers rather than names, personal life is reduced to a minimum, the 'One State' is surrounded by a Green Wall, citizens march in ranks of four (in Ivan Denisovich's camp there is a rule, hardly enforceable at it happens, that the prisoners move around in groups of four or five when in the compound [Paris, p. 95; Willetts, p. 118], and, of course, they are marched and searched in ranks of five). The mathematical gymnastics so evident in Zamyatin's anti-Utopian satire have become anything but a joke in Ivan Denisovich's world, where every gramme of bread is measured, every bowl of gruel.

In sum, just as it would be doing Zamyatin a disservice to see his novel first and foremost as a tract directed against totalitarianism *avant la parole*, so too it would be parochial to view *Ivan Denisovich* as solely an indictment of Stalinism. That the work lacks the predictive quality, which Bullock rather implies is one of the key criteria for Modernist art, may be so; that the book has a Modernist dimension, reinforced by historical experience, seems equally valid.

II. Epic Traits and the Tolstoy Dimension

When one surveys Solzhenitsyn's career as a whole, it is easy to discern his close affinities with Tolstoy. In addition to his boundless energy, his uncompromising commitment to social and moral issues, his preparedness to engage in public debate on the political and social issues of the day, there are the more specifically literary parallels. Solzhenitsyn can create vivid and vital characters. His larger works obviously merit the term 'epic', and here we can see a fascinating parallel between the development of the nineteenth-century master and Solzhenitsyn: in writing *War and Peace*, Tolstoy felt that he had to 'go back' a half-century to explain Russia's current predicament, and Solzhenitsyn does the same in *The Red Wheel* (which introduces Tolstoy as a character), striving as he does to portray how, in his eyes, Russia fell prey to an alien and damaging ideology. Many critics of Solzhenitsyn's larger works have discussed the Tolstoy connection, but there was mention of Tolstoy even with the publication of *Ivan Denisovich*. (As we have noted earlier, some of such commentary, particularly that involving charges of 'karataevshchina', had not always been complimentary.) In the case of the Russian critics, especially at the outset, linking Solzhenitsyn with Tolstoy could be seen in part as an attempt to give the new writer an aura of respectability as he embarked on a highly controversial, even dangerous, topic. Such would be the case with Ermilov's review of the work. But other critics, with no axe to grind, also seized on Tolstoy as Solzhenitsyn's role model. Kathryn Feuer, in an examination primarily of Solzhenitsyn's major novels, writes:

> In several ways Tolstoy seems to have provided models for Solzhenitsyn's fiction. Since a writer's first published work is usually significant of his elective affinities, it is worth noting that the account of a day in the life of Ivan Denisovich recalls Tolstoy's 'The Woodfelling' in its chief organizing devices: men of various class and attitude, caught in a common situation of stress which belongs to and is yet outside the ordinary life of their society, joined together by membership in a group within the larger whole, conducted through a day which begins before dawn and ends in moonlight,

with the position and heat of the sun used to define forward
movement and also to demarcate shifts in mood or focus.[1]

Tolstoy, Solzhenitsyn recalled, had stated that a novel could deal with a
century of European history or could equally treat of a single day in the life
of a peasant. Tolstoy's *History of Yesterday*, the abortive work of 1851,
failed where Solzhenitsyn succeeded. Tvardovsky likened *Ivan Denisovich*
to Tolstoy's moral tales.[2] When Tolstoy read Homer he was so caught by
his artistry that he was moved to teach himself Greek so as to appreciate
him in the original. The links between Homer and Tolstoy's art have been
frequently commented upon: Tolstoy was particularly taken with the oral
and graphic qualities of the *Iliad*. These are, of course, echoed in the use of
skaz in *Ivan Denisovich* and in the often cited authenticity which the author
generates. Solzhenitsyn seems to have been similarly moved by *War and
Peace*, which he apparently first read at the age of ten,[3] and as we have
already noted, Solzhenitsyn followed a similar path to Tolstoy in producing
his own conventional epic in order to come to terms with Russia's history.

There is also, as noted above, the question of 'karataevshchina'.

We will explore the Tolstoyan qualities of *Ivan Denisovich* primarily in
terms of the epic and character-creation.

To consider *Ivan Denisovich* an epic work we need to be clear about what
we mean by the term. Length alone is irrelevant. (Dostoevsky's *The Brothers
Karamazov* is some seven hundred pages long, but is not an epic; Blok's
poem *The Twelve* – 335 lines long – is). The classic epics were concerned
in the main with some key episode or episodes in national history, often with
the establishment of a new society, with issues of national identity and
survival, and with mortals locked in combat with the gods. Heroes were at
times in conflict also with close relatives, even inadvertently. They were
often imprisoned far from home by forces they could not control. Naturally,
these common traits of the epic frequently involve a lengthy narrative, vast
crowds and physical prowess; but of more significance is the impression of
an entire society, of key individuals within that society, who are essential
for its survival, and at least an *impression* of history, if not a full-blown
attempt to come to terms with history, and to understand its mechanisms.
All this presupposes that history can be made sense of, and even implies a
linear and/or teleological perception of history. That many writers in the
modern world reject the possibility of making sense of history, explains the
relative dearth of aesthetically convincing 'straight' epic works and the
existence of the mock epic.

For a short work – we note that it is designated a *povest'* rather than a *roman*
– *Ivan Denisovich* contains an extraordinarily large number of characters.
Nearly thirty are designated by a proper name or a nickname, and there are

approximately eighty individuals mentioned throughout the text, if we include people who figure in the various *zeks*' biographies: for instance, Ivan's wife, his two daughters and his dead son. Ivan's work team consists of twenty-four individuals, the chief among these being: the hero himself, Tyurin, Buynovsky, Tsezar, Fetyukov, Gopchik, Alyoshka, Klevshin, Kildigs, Pavlo, Panteleyev, the two Estonians, one of whom, Eino, is addressed by name when Ivan borrows tobacco from him (Paris, p. 62; Willetts, p. 73), and Yermolaev, who is introduced only towards the end of the novel, over supper (Paris, p. 99; Willetts, p. 123). Few prisoners are designated only by their serial numbers. In addition, Solzhenitsyn rarely misses the opportunity of informing the reader of a character's ethnic origins: the prisoner who falls asleep on the construction site and keeps everyone behind is a Moldavian, and he is kicked by a Hungarian. The result is that we have a rich and multi-cultural slice of humanity. This, of course, represents only a small segment of the human life in the camp, but in true epic style, we are never allowed to forget the magnitude of the world to which we have been admitted. There are five hundred men in Ivan's column of convict labourers marched out to the building site; and on the return journey they race against a column of three hundred men from the engineering works. At the guardhouse outside the camp compound we are told that five roads meet, and that an hour earlier these had all been crowded with other work parties (*chasom ran'she na nikh vse ob"ekty tolpilis'* (Paris, p. 88; Willetts, p. 108). In a previous chapter we noted how the prisoners' serial numbers alone give a fairly precise idea of the scale of the camp.

Solzhenitsyn's ability to convey within the confines of a short work a picture of vastness and a series of close-ups is in itself Tolstoyan. What is equally worthy of the nineteenth-century master is the manner in which he invests even the seemingly least significant character with a life and an identity beyond the immediate demands of the plot. When Ivan and Kildigs go off to filch the tarred paper to keep the heat in the building they are working on, we have a view of the site given in pure *skaz* (Ivan's speech) followed by the hero's encounter with a man he is slightly familiar with. The Willetts translation has 'Huge their work site was, a country walk from one side to the other' (Willetts, p. 45); the original is: *Ikh'ego ob"ekta zona zdorová – poka-a proidësh' cherezo vsiu!* (Paris, p. 41). Then Ivan sees a man from another gang whom he knows and offers him some advice about thawing out the frozen ground before digging it. But the important stylistic point about this episode is that the man, whom we will never meet again, is 'from Vyatka' (a *viatich*). One is tempted to read significance into the fact that this former place of exile under the Tsars (Herzen, for example, enjoyed its hospitality) was renamed Kirov after the assassination of the Leningrad Party boss in 1934. Hence it denotes the start of the Great Purges. Ivan and/or the narrator have not taken on board the new Soviet name. What is indisputable is that the detail adds to the sense of community inherent in the encounter – even the smallest character, no less than Buynovsky, Ivan and a host of others, has a former life and a former environment.

Similarly, in the news Ivan has from home about the depopulation of the village, the two remaining males are named and other details supplied: 'The foreman Zakhar Vasilievich and the carpenter Tikhon, eighty-four years old, got married recently, and has children already' (Paris, p. 31; Willetts, p. 33). A few short paragraphs earlier Ivan has recalled how war broke out – folk came back from Polomnya from mass and announced it. In this instance the reference to Polomnya is picked up on near the end of the novel, when Ivan tells Alyoshka the Baptist about the well-heeled priest there who pays child maintenance to three women and lives with a fourth family (Paris, p. 117; Willetts, p. 146).

Another telling example of the smallest of characters taking on a life of his/her own beyond the immediate demands of the plot occurs when Tyurin is telling the story of his own attempts to avoid the authorities after his father is arrested as a kulak. His biography is criss-crossed with coincidence: he is dishonourably discharged from the army for his class origins; later, in a transit prison in 1938, he meets up with his old platoon commander, who had been given a 10-year sentence, and learns from him that both his old CO and the political commissar had been shot in 1937. Six female students hide him when he boards a train illegally to try and make it back home. We are given just a few physical details of one of them as she tries to get some boiling water at the station and Tyurin helps her: 'A girl wearing a blue blouse carrying a two-litre kettle, but she was scared of going up to the boiler. She had podgy little legs, and might get scalded or trodden on' (Paris, p. 63; Willetts, p. 74). He later meets one of them, arrested in 1935 in the wake of the Kirov assassination, and is able to repay her by getting her an easier job in the camp in the tailor's shop.

The mention of the 'Kirov wave' of arrests takes us back to the 'man from Vyatka'. Such cross-referencing reinforces the notion of a riven community, and more particularly gives an impression of sweep and expanse, as well as of vitality and individuality. At the same time there is not a trace of Solzhenitsyn endeavouring to contrive his tale. Readers of Pasternak's *Doctor Zhivago* have frequently felt ill at ease with the ubiquitous coincidences in the text. Pasternak replied in a letter to Stephen Spender that in engineering so many chance encounters he was trying to express 'the liberty of being, its verisimilitude touching, adjoining improbability' (his English).[4] It could be argued that *Ivan Denisovich* performs precisely this feat – in the most improbable, or, depending on your point of view, mundane of settings, and without taxing the reader's willing suspension of disbelief. Moreover, one notes that the chance encounters with former friends or relatives which involve retribution or acts of gratitude are a hall-mark of the epic. Solzhenitsyn's characters, unlike Homer's or Virgil's, may not reappear in disguise or so physically changed as to deceive former acquaintances, but the changed circumstances they find themselves in are no less dramatic.

In what ways do *Ivan Denisovich*'s heroes find themselves in combat with god-like forces? To what extent are they redolent of muscle-bound warriors? Ivan's toil seems to have little to do with the Protestant work ethic, still less to do with officially sanctioned socialist obligations, and a great deal to do with notions established in Homer's epics and adopted by Tolstoy. Derived from Indo-European notions of justice the Greek epic contains the idea that each being is given a particular fate (*moira*) which has clearly defined boundaries. The notion is close to the Russian *dolia* (allotted fate, share) rather than *sud'ba* (fate, judgement). A man's *moira* can determine his social standing as well as his ultimate end, his death. These boundaries should never be crossed. Thus, man's courage and energy should not be directed towards exceeding the limits of his condition, but in bearing it with style, pride and dignity. He should acquire fame within the limits of his *moira*. If, usually at the bidding of some god or goddess, he is persuaded to commit an act of excess (*hubris*), he will be punished by divine vengeance (personified as Nemesis). These considerations provide us with a perfect framework for explaining Ivan Denisovich's behaviour, and that of many other characters in the book. One notes Buynovsky's act of *hubris* when he protests at being made to remove some outer clothing, and achieves nothing but ten days in the cells for his pains (Paris, p. 27; Willetts, pp. 27-8).

The most important character in the work, after Ivan himself, is his foreman (*brigadir*), Andrei Prokofievich Tyurin, and while he clearly has human limitations, in Ivan's eyes he attains a god-like status.

> The foreman in the camp is everything: a good foreman will give you a second life, a bad foreman will drive you into a wooden overcoat. Shukhov had known Andrei Prokofievich from Ust-Izhma, only he hadn't been in his team there. But when from Ust-Izhma, from the general camp, they had shifted all those inside under Article 58 here, to the labour camp – then Tyurin had picked him up. With the boss of the camp, with the Production Planning Section, the managers or the engineers Shukhov had no business: everywhere it was his foreman who stood up for him, the foreman had a chest of steel. Yet he only had to cock an eyebrow or lift his finger, and you did his bidding at the double.
>
> (Paris, p. 34; Willetts, p. 36)

Near the beginning of the story, we are told that Tyurin may have interceded on Ivan's behalf when the Tartar guard punishes him, if he had been present; and right at the end of the work, Tyurin tries to save Buynovsky from his first night in the punishment cell by pretending not to remember the unfortunate man's serial number. The status of the foreman is determined by the camp system itself, since a team's rations are linked to its work output, and the foreman has to negotiate the work rates as well as the particular tasks the team will be assigned to. After Tyurin has finished telling his story during their break and has ordered them all back to work, we are informed, either through Ivan's thought processes or the will o' the wisp narrator: 'There's the team for you (*Vot eto ono i est' – brigada*). Even in work time the boss can't get a poor bloody worker (*rabotiaga*) to move himself, but a foreman even during a break only has to say work – and that means work. Because he's the one that feeds you, the foreman is. And he doesn't force you to do anything for nothing, either' (Paris, p. 64; Willetts, p. 76). Just a few paragraphs later Pavlo, the deputy foreman, happily volunteers to make mortar when Tyurin volunteers to lay blocks, and we have a near-repeat of the words just quoted: 'That's the team for you! (*Vot ono i est' brigada!*) [...] Doing something for the foreman – that's different!' (Paris, p. 65; Willetts, p. 77).

Consider the physical description we have of Tyurin: 'The foreman's face is covered in huge pock-marks, from small-pox. He stands into the wind – won't even wince, the skin on his face is like oak bark.' (*Litso u brigadira v riabinakh krupnykh, ot ospy. Stoit protiv vetra, – ne pomorshchitsia, kozha na litse – kak kora dubovaia,* Paris, p. 34; Willetts, p. 37). The more or less literal translation offered here is awkwardly tautological in a way that the Russian is not, and in retaining the present tense tries to highlight the immediacy and graphic qualities of the original. Such a picture would not be out of place in many a Socialist Realist novel (one thinks of the 'gimlet eyes' and 'steel jaw' of the hero in Serafimovich's over-rated classic of the Civil War *The Iron Flood*). This type of resilience, linked as it is with the natural elements, is echoed elsewhere in the novel: at the very beginning of the work Ivan remembers what his first-ever foreman, Kuzyomin, told him about 'the law of the *taiga*' by which those who lick out others' bowls, keep running to the sick-bay or going to inform, will die first (Paris, pp. 7-8; Willetts, p. 1-2). Such strength then goes hand-in-hand with morality and human dignity – one recalls Tyurin's selflessness (helping the girl with the boiling water, saving his kid brother); or Pavlo, the deputy foreman, giving Buynovsky an extra bowl of kasha – rightly, in Ivan's opinion, for no other reason than that the Captain has not yet learned how to survive in the camp.

Whilst there are severe limits to Tyurin's powers, and ultimately he is a *zek* like any other, his social achievements are considerable in the way he does his best for his team. Inevitably this leads him into conflicts: most dramatically with Der, the convict overseer and trusty, who threatens to report Tyurin for the misappropriated tarred paper. His face contorted and his whole body shaking, Tyurin threatens to kill him (Paris, p. 71; Willetts, pp. 85-6). Pavlo and Klevshin, without uttering a word, back him up. The episode is dealt with in a series of short, one-sentence and even one-word paragraphs which strip away any metaphysical notions: here we have a simple enactment of man's primeval physicality, no different from battle scenes in *War and Peace* where elemental violence is seen to have its attractions for its own sake.

Tyurin's towering authority is to be seen in the other foremen and their deputies as well, as when the Moldavian is beaten by his deputy foreman, after the guard has turned his rifle butt, presumably to strike the miscreant himself. The foremen's standing derives from their personal qualities rather than from the position to which they have been appointed (which is the case with the warders), and unlike the overseers – even the most brutal, like Volkovoi – they command respect, not just instil fear. Respect and personal moral strength are qualities accessible to all in the camp. In this way Ivan Denisovich, through his skill and tenacity as a workman, momentarily attains equality with Tyurin. Significantly, battle with the elements also plays a part in his ascent. (One might add that not all writers on camp themes were so positive about brigade leaders, Varlam Shalamov for one.)

> Shukhov and the other bricklayers stopped feeling the frost. From the fast work taking hold of them from the word go the first bit of heat ran through them – that bit of heat that makes you wet underneath your jacket, and your sleeveless coat, underneath your overshirt and undershirt. They didn't stop for an instant, and just rushed on with the laying further and further. An hour later the second bit of heat got through to them – the one that makes the sweat dry out. The frost wasn't getting at their feet, that was the main thing, and nothing else, not even that light breeze which kept at them, could take their thoughts off the bricklaying [...]
> From time to time the foreman would shout 'Morta-ar!' And Shukhov did his own version: 'Morta-ar!' He who puts his back into his work also becomes a sort of foreman over his neighbours.
>
> (Paris, pp. 68-9; Willetts, p. 82)

Immediately following this passage we find Ivan chasing up even Buynovsky (*Shukhov ego podgonial legon'ko: 'Kavtorang, pobystrei!'*). At the end of the shift Ivan has gained full equality with Tyurin: 'Get going, foreman! Get going, you're more needed there! – (Shukhov usually called him Andrei Prokofievich, but now by means of his work he was equal with the foreman [*no seichas svoei rabotoi on s brigadirom sravnialsia*]. Not that he had thought like that: "Now I'm equal", but he simply felt that's how it was.)' (Paris, p. 76; Willetts, p. 92). One could draw parallels here with the celebrated hay-making scene in *Anna Karenina*, when Levin, the land-owner, becomes as one with his peasants on the estate.

Indeed, the whole episode of building the wall can be construed in terms of the traditions of the great epics. Were it not for this and for the considerations that we raised in the previous chapter, it would be the easiest thing in the world to pass this key passage off as no more than Socialist Realism. As it is, such writing – even when executed by masters such as Solzhenitsyn, Tolstoy and many others – is vulnerable to parody; more worryingly, the truth it portrays, as identified in our epigraph, is open to the most evil abuse: *Arbeit macht frei* was inscribed over the gates of Dachau concentration camp.[5]

The struggle that the prisoners have with the system, with their wretched diet, the rules and the camp authorities, is obvious. These epic heroes find themselves at the mercy of the modern gods of the all-pervading ideology and totalitarianism under which all Soviet citizens laboured.Yet overriding this is the struggle which all the humans in the novel conduct with the natural elements.

The struggle begins in the first paragraph, where there is two fingers of ice on the windows and it is too cold for the warder to go on sounding reveille for long. Ivan has been unable to get warm all night and there is a web of hoar frost where the walls of the hut meet the ceiling. The Russian original here is more curt and stark than the Willetts translation: *pautina belaia. Inei.* (Paris, p. 8; Willetts, p. 2) concludes the paragraph. Shortly after this comes the mention of the new site they may be assigned to, where the snow would be knee-deep and they would have no chance of getting warm for the first month. The two mentions of the thermometer outside – strategically positioned in a place where it will not fall too low – tells us a lot: that according to the rules if the temperature is lower than minus 41° C the *zek*s will not have to work. When we are informed that it is nowhere near 40° (Paris, p. 11; Willetts, p. 6), it is left unclear whether Ivan has been able to read the thermometer or feels what the temperature is. It only turns out to be the latter at the second mention of the thermometer, when one of the *zek*s has to shin up the pole to read it (Paris, p. 12; Willetts, p. 7). According to it, the temperature is 27.5° below. So Ivan is able to sense what others have to find out by scientific investigation (he shows similar perspicacity in being able to assess the weight of his bread rations); but, the irony is that they do not trust the technology... Yet the thermometer theme is taken up again in the sick-bay, where Ivan's temperature is measured as 37.2°, 'neither one thing nor the other', as the medical orderly, Vdovushkin, tells him (Paris, p. 20; Willetts, p. 18). As Ivan leaves without a word, we have, in two terse paragraphs, an excellent example of blending between the words of an omniscient narrator and the hero's unuttered thoughts:

> When will a warm [man] really understand a cold [man]?
> The frost squeezed him. The frost grabbed Shukhov pain-
> fully in a sharp mist and made him start coughing. In the frost
> it was twenty-seven, in Shukhov thirty-seven. Now it's dog
> eat dog.
>
> (*Tëplyi ziablogo razve kogda poimët?*
> *Moroz zhal. Moroz edkoi mglitsei bol'no okhvatil Shukhova i*
> *vynudil ego zakashliat'sia. V moroze bylo dvadtsat' sem', v*
> *Shukhove tridtsat' sem'. Teper' kto kogo.*)
>
> (Paris, p. 20; Willetts, p. 18)

As they leave the hut to assemble for work parade we learn that it is still dark, though the sky is green and light (*zelenelo i svetlelo*) from the east. 'And a thin, evil [or, nasty, vicious] breeze kept at them from the east' (*I tonkii, zloi potiagival s voskhoda veterok*, Paris, p. 23; Willetts, p. 21). These words concerning the breeze are closely echoed as the column sets off for the site (Paris, p. 29; Willetts, p. 30) and again during the wall-building scene (Paris, p. 69; Willetts, p. 82). Moreover, one notes here that the word for 'east' is the archaic *voskhod*, nowadays used exclusively to mean 'sunrise', thus strengthening the epic flavour. Once the column sets off 'as if to a funeral' (*kak na pokhorony*, Paris, p. 30; Willetts, p. 31) there is reference to the snow and the wind, and the guards' shouts die out – unlike the prisoners, they are not allowed to wear face cloths and they cannot bear the cold either. There is even a hint of sympathy for the guards: 'Theirs was a pretty rotten job too' (*Tozhe sluzhba nevazhnaia...*, Paris, p. 30; Willetts, p. 31), the colloquial use of the adjective here suggesting Ivan's thought processes rather than the voice of an omniscient narrator (thus, another good example of 'dual voice' or 'style indirecte libre', as discussed towards the end of the overview of Soviet responses in Chapter Two, Part One).

In striving to forget the cold and hunger, Ivan directs his thoughts to his home village, but it is worth noting that here too there is a good deal of emphasis on the turning of the seasons and the time of year, with months named and contemplation of his remaining time in the camp, 'a winter and summer, and another winter and summer' (*zimu-leto da zimu-leto*, Paris, p. 32; Willetts, p. 34).

The first break in the natural elements comes when the column arrives outside the site and a big red sun rises as if in 'a mist' (*mgla*, Paris, p. 33; Willetts, p. 35 has 'fog'). Shortly after this, there is a deliberate juxtaposition of Shukhov's sorry physical state with that of his foreman, as the hero ponders his own aches and pains and feels where the cold has penetrated (his hands and the toes of his left foot). His foreman though is big in the shoulders (*v plechakh zdorov*) and 'has a broad face' (*obraz u nego shirokii*, Paris, p. 34; Willetts, p. 36). One is tempted to see the foreman as the incarnation of the sun, and Ivan as the insubstantial mist around it. It is also significant that the word *obraz* is used for 'face' here: 'image' or 'form' would be the more usual meaning, and again the connotations are epic and even biblical. Immediately following this, we have the passage already cited to the effect that the foreman (like the sun) is very much the life-giver as far as his team are concerned. The 'evil breeze' (*zloi veterok*) is still there.

A dim red sun rises over the site and Ivan and his workmates are able to get a little warm in the automobile repair shop, while their work assignment is being issued; yet the talk turns to the natural elements again. Kildigs complains that they have not had a blizzard (*buran*) all winter (Paris, p. 38; Willetts, p. 42). Again it is worth noting the ellipsis here and the direct speech which are bound to be lost in translation: '*Da... buranov... buranov... – perevzdokhnula brigada.*'

The Willetts version has: 'The gang all sighed for the blizzards they hadn't had.' The convicts' longing for bad weather is at first puzzling, and then ironic to the point of comedy, given the climatic conditions we have witnessed so far. It turns out that during blizzards the prisoners cannot be taken out to work, not for humanitarian reasons, but so that they do not try to escape, even though they would not get far (Paris, p. 39; Willetts, pp. 42-3). We quickly learn in the same passage that in fact the prisoners are no better off because of such blizzards, since coal and flour cannot be delivered to the camp regularly, so there is no warmth or bread, and any work that is missed will mean Sunday working for them to catch up. The *zeks*' love of blizzards then is essentially illogical. The reader is left to register subconsciously that the natural elements are the ultimate arbiter, and that blizzards are a just revenge for the unnatural, man-made world discussed in the previous chapter, where searchlights outshine the stars. The convicts' fondness for the snow is expressed in their affectionate terminology: *mater'ial'chik* and *snezhok* (Paris, p. 39; Willetts, p. 43).

The sun, this time in a fog (*tuman*), is mentioned again when Ivan and Kildigs go off to fetch the tarred paper, and this time it is linked with fence posts, with Ivan's partner making a joke about posts being all right as long as they do not have barbed wire strung between them (Paris, p. 41; Willetts, p. 45). Once more, what superficially seems an insignificant detail is charged with meaning: the two *zeks* are not sure if they are posts that they see (so the uncertainty factor raises its head), but they are certain of the sun's presence; and for anyone with knowledge of Pushkin and Mandelshtam – and Ivan emphatically is not – the sun has strong connotations of justice. Thus, Kildigs' joke conveys more to the reader than to Ivan.

The interlocking of heroic spirit and the natural elements is deftly spelled out in the short paragraph describing the shell of the power-house that team 104 is to work on (Paris, p. 43; Willetts, p. 48). It stands 'like a grey skeleton, in the snow, abandoned. But now the 104th had arrived. And what kept its souls together? (*I v chëm eë dushi derzhatsia?*) – empty trousers tied up with canvas belts; frost crackling (*morozka treshchit*); no heater, not a spark of fire. But anyway the 104th had arrived – and life was starting again (*i opiat' zhizn' nachinaetsia*).' Just a few pages later the sun has risen higher in the sky and the mist has gone. The posts that Kildigs joked about have also disappeared from view, we are told (Paris, p. 45; Willetts, p. 51). So it would seem that life and justice are winning out over imprisonment. Here the sun is described as 'crimson' (*alyi*) rather than simply 'red' (*krasnyi*), as hitherto. On the surface, Ivan's comment that the sun used to warm the cow's flanks in January is suitably *à propos* of nothing, for an inarticulate peasant, but it clearly recalls the hero's former life, and once again stresses for the reader the connotations of justice. The diminutives *solnyshko* and *korovka* for 'sun' and 'cow' underscore Ivan's rustic origins in a way that is lost in translation. A little later, Buynovsky is to joke that Soviet power has decreed that the sun is at its highest at one o'clock, not noon (Paris, p. 48; Willetts, p. 54). Ivan's mental response to this is somewhat more ambiguous than a translation can convey: *Neuzh i solntse ikhim dekretam podchiniaetsia?* The colloquial first and fourth words here obviously denote Ivan's speech patterns, but is he really saying, as the Willetts version has it, 'As if the sun would obey their decrees!'? The original has a question mark rather than an exclamation mark, and more literally could be rendered as 'Can the sun really submit to their decrees?'. Ivan is still growing in self-assurance at this stage of the story. His lack of education and his general superstition mean that at this point his awe is equally divided between the Soviet system and the natural elements.

By lunchtime Ivan estimates that it is only minus 18° C (Paris, p. 51; Willetts, p. 59), and he looks at the sun to check out the 'captain's decree', an action which rather supports the view that he is still a long way from placing the power of nature above the power of the Soviet system. There have been several mentions of the wind so far, but a fuller one comes with the hooter signalling dinner: 'The wind whistles over the bare steppe – in summer dryish (*sukhoveinyi*), in winter frosty' (Paris, p. 52; Willetts, p. 61), and we are informed that nothing ever grows on the steppe, especially inside four wire fences. Often the word for wind is diminutivised in the text (*veterok*), but not on this occasion, and it opens a lengthy paragraph recounting the stark struggle for existence that is the *zek*'s:

> Wheat grows only in the bread-cutting shop, oats grow ears in the food stores. And even if you break your back working, even if you lie down on your belly – you still won't get anything to eat out of the ground, you won't get any more than the boss man allots you. And you won't even get that, given all the cooks, their helpers and the trusties between it and you. They steal here, and they steal in the compound, and even before it gets there they steal in the stores. And all those who steal, don't slog away themselves with a pickaxe. But you slog away, and take what you're given. And move away from the hatch.
>
> If you can do someone, screw someone (*Kto kogo smozhet, tot togo i glozhet*).   (Paris, pp. 52-3; Willetts, p. 61).

In this passage we see a mingling of the forces which oppress the convict: the natural elements, the man-made system and then the dishonesty of the individuals who operate the system. The full resonances are hard to capture in English: 'wheat' in the original is *khleb* (bread, or crops or cereal) and is repeated in 'bread-cutting shop' (*khleborezka*). 'Helpers' (*shestërki*) and 'trusties' (*pridurki*) are words from the criminal world, *shestërka* (from the verb *shesterit'*, to oblige, or dance attendance on) meaning either a lackey or a petty thief. The aphoristic one-sentence paragraph is aptly rendered by Willetts, though he dispenses with the rhyme of the original, as 'It's dog eat dog here' (p. 61).

During lunch there is practically no mention of the natural elements, but when Ivan takes Tsezar's meal to him in the office he is told to shut the door against the cold, and much is made of the artificial warmth of the stove. Moreover, we have a reference to the sun – which looked cold and hostile when the men were working on the power station, but viewed through the window now seems more congenial to Ivan : (*igralo uzhe ne zlo* [...] *a veselo*, Paris, p. 58; Willetts, p. 68). When he returns to the building they are working on, it seems quite dark inside after he has been out in the sun, and 'it was a bit damper somehow' (or 'rawer') (*syrovatei kak-to*, Paris, p. 60; Willetts, p. 70). This presages the news that the foreman has negotiated a good rate, in terms of rations, for his gang and then the foreman's long story about his own experiences on the run as the son of a kulak.

The human spirit really defeats the adverse weather conditions once work is in full swing. Just before this we are informed that the sun is shining so much (*solntse iaro bleshchet*, Paris, p. 65; Willetts, p. 78) that you cannot look into it, yet at the opening of the long introductory paragraph to the work scene Ivan does not see the sun shining on the snow (Paris, p. 66; Willetts, pp. 78-9). Ice is hacked off the partially built wall, and there is a mention of the sun on the snow, but Ivan is entirely absorbed in the blocklaying. One notes that now it is not the convicts who are at the mercy of the elements, but the mortar that they are using, for if they do not work quickly enough with it, it will freeze in the barrows. By contrast, Ivan and his colleagues are working up quite a sweat, as we noted above. After the near-violent confrontation between Der and Tyurin, the former backs off and makes his way to the office to get warm (*V kontoru, gret'sia*, Paris, p. 73; Willetts, p. 87), once again the Russian original being more terse and direct than English idiom can comfortably allow for. And soon after this there is a folksy description of the sun getting low in the sky, a red patch descending into a greyish fog (*Da, solnyshko na zakhode. S krasninkoi zakhodit i v tuman vrode by seden'kii*, Paris, p. 73; Willetts, p. 88), and soon Ivan is feeling the cold again. However, this does not prevent him from doing some voluntary, frenzied 'overtime' so that the mortar which has already been mixed will not be wasted.

By the time the gangs are assembled at the end of the shift, the moon is up. Significantly, it is referred to in affectionate, folksy terms, which contrast with the manner in which the natural elements were described at the start of the novel: '[Ivan] looked behind – that there moon, little father, frowned crimson, and had already come out full up in the sky' (*oglianulsia – a mesiats-to, batiushka, nakhmurilsia bagrovo, uzh na nebo ves' vylez*, Paris, p. 78; Willetts, p. 94). Ivan's observations here prefix the enchanting superstition that he relates to Buynovsky about God crumbling up the moon each month to make stars. While they wait for the count of prisoners to tally there is a reference to Tsezar's 'black moustache all covered in hoar frost' (Paris, p. 81; Willetts, p. 98). Once more the Russian is able to do in one word what it takes half a dozen to achieve in English: *obyndevet'* means 'to get covered in hoar frost'. Immediately following this, we have a near repetition of the phrase to the effect that a warm man cannot understand a cold one. Now the elements are gaining the upper hand once again, and Ivan's feelings are reported to us direct, as the gangs are forced to wait for the Moldavian prisoner:

> Now spite took hold of the whole crowd and of Shukhov too [...] The sky's dark now, reckon the light must be coming from the moon, stars are gone, the frost is gathering its night-time strength.   (Paris, p. 81; Willetts, p. 99)

By the time the latecomer is found, the moon is 'shining at full strength' and the 'crimsonness has gone from it' (Paris, p. 83; Willetts, p. 102); yet while the cold is now getting at the prisoners again, what is worse is that their evening has been spoilt (Paris, p. 84; Willetts, p. 102). The close-up we have had of Ivan's inner world, which could easily be duplicated in many of the other forced labourers, emphasises a degree of individual freedom and an ability to transcend the vicissitudes of the natural world, which still linger on in them. They are now in a position to inconvenience the guards, by taking their time marching back to the camp. Moreover, Ivan has now forgotten all about his aches and pains of the morning, and sees no point now in going to the sick-bay (Paris, p. 86; Willetts, p. 105). The view of the camp stresses that it is the same as they left it, but now with the artificial lights, not so much rivalling the stars, as likened to the sun (Paris, p. 87; Willetts, pp. 107-8). Once Ivan has been searched and is about to re-enter the camp, there is another description of the moon and the frost, this time more neutral, possibly reflecting Ivan's relief at smuggling the hack-saw blade in successfully: 'The moon rode (*vykatyval*) still higher, and in the white, bright night the frost was coming on (*nastaivalsia*)' (Paris, p. 91; Willetts, p. 111). The two verbs here have a homely quality to them, the second one used particularly of brewing up tea or distilling vodka. At the last count, as they go through the camp gates, one paragraph draws together practically all the aspects of Ivan's epic struggle: cold and hunger; his expressions of freedom together with the acceptance of his fate; his capacity for concentrating on a single moment in his daily existence (*byt*) rather than contemplating a whole life (*zhizn'*) (with all its imponderables):

> Here at this evening count, returning through the camp gates, for the convict, after a whole day blown about by the wind, frozen through and starved (*obvetren, vymerz, vygolodal*), more than anything just a ladleful of scalding-hot, thin cabbage soup is now like rain in a drought, – he'll draw it in to the last drop in one go. Now this ladleful is dearer to him than freedom (*volia*), dearer than all his former life and all his future life (*zhizn'*).   (Paris, p. 91; Willetts, p. 112)

The notion is picked up on later, during the evening meal, when the hero reflects on the 'short instant' (*mig korotkii*) which the convict lives for (Paris, p. 101; Willetts, p. 126).

The epic dimension is reinforced in the very next paragraph, which has the convicts returning 'like warriors from a campaign' (*kak voiny s pokhoda*, Paris, p. 91; Willetts, p. 112), and the following one-sentence paragraph provides yet another of those seemingly incidental details, which in fact are bursting with significance: 'The trusty from the staff hut is scared to look at the wave of entering convicts' (*Pridurku ot shtabnogo baraka smotret' na val vkhodiashchikh zekov – strashno*). The original is slightly ambiguous in that the trusty is either too afraid to look or feels afraid as he looks. The word for 'wave' (*val*) is more resonant than the English here – 'billow' or 'tidal wave' might be more precise, and there are connotations of *deviatyi val*, the ninth wave, which according to the sailor's superstition, is most likely to engulf the ship (see, for example, Erenburg's 1951 novel of that title, or nearer home, lines in Tennyson's *Idylls of the King: The Coming of Arthur*). Clearly, the convicts have grown in confidence and power as a result of their engagement with the climate, and others with even a small privileged position are insecure. There are obvious parallels here with the vulnerability or otherwise of the Soviet system overall. Historians have wondered at how a nation capable of defeating Nazism could be so cowered by domestic tyranny. Solzhenitsyn has pondered the issue in other works: in *The Gulag Archipelago* he speculates as to how far the purges could have gone if ordinary people had not simply offered armed resistence to the squads of secret policemen who went out on their nightly errands. He concludes:

> If... if.... We didn't love freedom enough. And even more –
> we had no awareness of the real situation. We spent our-
> selves in one unrestrained outburst in 1917, and then we
> *hurried* to submit. We submitted *with pleasure!*[6]

References to the natural elements thin out now, especially when Ivan saves a place for Tsezar in the parcel queue, but there is a mention of it getting brighter outside in the moonlight, when the lights have dimmed, and each lamp outside shines like a rainbow (*raduzhno*) because of the frost or dirt on it (Paris, p. 96; Willetts, p. 119). As we noted above, Ivan lives for the brief instant as he savours his evening meal, but this moment gives him the physical and spiritual strength to survive ('We'll survive!' *Perezhivëm!*, p. 101; Willetts, p. 126). He also contemplates at some length the old prisoner Yu-81, who himself acquires certain epic traits in his resilience to his harsh life (his face is like dark, chiselled stone, his hands are large and cracked and black [Paris, p. 102; Willetts, p. 127]). Thus, it is not surprising that when he emerges from the mess hall, Ivan sees the natural elements in a more congenial light: the moon is pure and white (*chistyi, belyi*) and here and there the stars are at their brightest (Paris, p. 102; Willetts, p. 128). He has heard that it will be 30° below by evening and 40° by morning (Paris, p. 103; Willetts, p. 128). But there is no wind. Back in the hut there is still a 'snowy web' (*obmet' snezhnaia*, Paris, p. 109; Willetts, p. 135).

When Buynovsky is taken off to the punishment cell we are told that it must have been easier for him to have taken torpedo boats out into the stormy sea than to leave this friendly conversation (Paris, p. 110; Willetts, p. 138). The way that the ferocity of the climate fluctuates, depending on the spirits of its victims, is brought out again shortly afterwards during the evening roll-call: Ivan is first out of the hut, in order to be the first back and save Tsezar's food parcel from theft, so he jauntily asks the others if they have never seen a Siberian frost before and issues a folksy directive to them: 'Go out into the wolf's sun and get warm!' (*Vykhodi na volch'e solnyshko gret'sia!* p. 113; Willetts, p. 140). We are informed that 'wolf's sun' is what the peasants call the moonlight where Ivan comes from, and the whimsical, almost lyrical tone is expanded with a description of the white sky, with a touch of green in it (*s suzelen'iu*), bright, sparse stars and the white glistening snow – the lights 'exert little influence' (*malo vliiaiut*) now. The only significant allusion to the weather after this comes at the second roll-call (the damp floor and the icy wind from the passageway, Paris, p. 119; Willetts, pp. 148-9).

In sum, though the natural elements are the ultimate arbiter and offer serious challenges to all the characters no matter what their standing, the manner in which they are perceived can vary according to circumstances. Additionally, man's interaction with the wind and the cold as he performs his allotted task helps define his character and the extent of his personal triumph: *zek*s can return to the camp as 'warriors' and as a tidal wave, achieving the status of the natural elements themselves. Even within the confines of *moira*, there is enormous scope for personal development. Moreover, given that Solzhenitsyn invests even the lowliest character with a rich identity, there is an intriguing paradox in *Ivan Denisovich*, an optimism founded not on history, politics or human institutions, but on faith in the human spirit.

III. Peasants, Workers and Intellectuals

The title of this Chapter can be taken as a spoof on the numerous and worthy, if over-generalising, attempts by social scientists to establish an anatomy of the large and complex society of what was the Soviet Union. It is also to be taken as an indication that *Ivan Denisovich*, in one fell swoop, gives us a near-comprehensive picture of 'life', including Soviet life, utilising the kind of methods that led critics in the case of Tolstoy to speak of a 'comprehensive vision' or a 'totality of objects'.[1] In ascribing such Tolstoyan qualities to Solzhenitsyn, we reject the suggestions voiced in some Soviet critical quarters, noted earlier, that the small format which Solzhenitsyn chose in some way limited his opportunities to create a fuller picture. Such a fuller picture, so the establishment Soviet view would have it, would have allowed the author to endow the prisoners with more hope and to have depicted some of the brighter side of Soviet life. As we tried to show in the previous chapter, if there is a brighter side to life in Ivan's world, it comes from sources which are utterly at variance with Soviet values and practices. Our examination of some of the chief characters in the work will certainly illustrate the 'social' aspect of Soviet life. It is also intended to explore further the methods of characterisation Solzhenitsyn employs and to shed more light on the *un*-Soviet nature of the work.

In an analysis of *War and Peace* R.F. Christian discusses Tolstoy's methods of characterisation as follows:

> In his endless revisions Tolstoy was guided by a few simple principles which he evolved for himself and which are typical of his approach to characterisation, which is the province above all in which he was to excel. Generally speaking he preferred to introduce his characters in situations and environments which were typical of their normal, everyday lives. He liked to do so too, where possible, in an indirect or oblique manner. In one version of the opening chapters of the book, the Viscount de Montemart is telling a story in Anna Scherer's salon before an assembly of guests who have been given only a perfunctory introduction. Tolstoy intended to interrupt the viscount's story to tell the reader more about

the main characters who form the audience, and indeed began to do so. Later, however, he crossed out his narrative description and scribbled in the margin: 'who listens and how' [...] As Tolstoy said at the age of twenty-two, echoing an observation of Lessing in the context of Homer: 'It seems to me that it is really impossible to *describe* a man, but it is possible to describe the effect he produces on me.'[2]

These comments apply equally well to Solzhenitsyn's method. We know from Solzhenitsyn's biography that several of the main characters in *Ivan Denisovich* are based on the author's first-hand observations. However, he channels his observations through the eyes of others – notably through Ivan, but sometimes through what some critics have identified as the second narrator. Moreover, the observations regarding a given character are passed on to the reader piecemeal, with little attempt at the traditional ordering of material, preferred by many a nineteenth-century realist – the opening chapter of George Eliot's *Middlemarch*, headed 'Miss Brooke', begins: 'Miss Brooke had that kind of beauty which seems...' and ushers in many pages concerning her biography and nature.

What I would call Solzhenitsyn's 'fragmented characterisation' has led Kodjak, for example, to argue uncompromisingly for the existence of a fully-fledged anonymous narrator-character, 'who, though present on every page of the book, remains unknown to the reader [...] One may conclude that he is a convict of very humble origins, on the same cultural level as Shukhov but of much broader experience, and that he has acquired during his life a knowledge of human nature which enables him to mediate between persons of different cultural backgrounds. He understands Shukhov intuitively, and portrays him without either idealizing or denigrating him'.[3] Thus, for Kodjak, 'Ivan Denisovich, as the narrator perceives him, is a complex figure: seemingly simple, even primitive in appearance, yet actually quite sophisticated and spiritually sublime'.[4] Given some of our foregoing remarks, one might take issue with Moody when he writes that 'Unlike Tolstoy, Solzhenitsyn does not build up his characters or the episodes in their lives from an accumulation of minute detail. The reader gains only a vague idea of Shukhov's appearance. Solzhenitsyn's technique of evoking a whole impression by means of a few carefully selected, emotionally neutral, facts is Chekhovian'.[5] The present critic takes the view, rather, that there is something of both Chekhov and Tolstoy in Solzhenitsyn's method; and *pace* Kodjak, Solzhenitsyn simply hovers between *skaz* and omniscient narrator, too frank and direct to be interested in creating characters whom we will never know, but adept at employing Pascal's dual voice.

What is undeniable is that Solzhenitsyn's portrait gallery was immediately accessible to his readers: 'Ivan Denisovich? That's me, sz-209. And I can give all the characters real names, not invented ones. Which camp?

Ukhta, 29th encampment. Or Steplag, Balkhash, 8th section'; 'It's the no. 8
mine in Vorkuta'; 'We were in the 104th brigade with you, lived in the same
hut'; 'Solzhenitsyn has not even changed Tyurin's name. I knew him, and
worked in the 104th brigade [...] I shall never forget the disciplinary officer,
Sodorov, introduced in the story as Volkovoi [...] I also knew Shukhov under
another name. There was one like him in every brigade'; 'The captain
suffered because of a gift – I suffered because of a letter from the USA. I was
dismissed from service in the navy'. These are brief quotes from the hundreds
of letters that Solzhenitsyn received when the book was published.[6] Such
remarks evidence the sort of authenticity in the work which in the West
unsophisticated aficionados of soap operas respond to, as for example, when
they send congratulations and gifts to fictional newly-weds they have come
to know on their television screens. In the context of the Soviet Union, what
was happening, quite simply, was that readers who for decades had been
fed a diet of literature telling them what life should be like, were now
savouring a work of literature which depicted a life with which they were
all too familiar – and yet a life which hitherto it had been dangerous even
to speak of, let alone to 'legitimise' in print.

As we noted earlier, Solzhenitsyn modelled his hero primarily on an individual he had known from his army days, who had not been in a camp. Working
from correspondence, interviews and published material, Michael Scammell
provides us with a more factual account of Solzhenitsyn's other sources:

> For many of his leading characters, Solzhenitsyn drew on
> prisoners he had known in Ekibastuz. The naval commander
> Buinovsky was based on Captain Boris Burkovsky from
> Leningrad – except for one episode during the morning
> roll-call which was taken from an incident that had happened
> to Vladimir Gershuni. Tsezar Markovich, the script writer,
> was based on a Muscovite, Lev Grossman [...] The early life
> of Tiurin, Ivan Denisovich's brigade leader and the son of a
> family of kulaks, was based on stories told to Solzhenitsyn
> by someone he later referred to (in *The Gulag Archipelago*)
> as Nikolai K (other parts of Tiurin's character were appar-
> ently modelled on someone else).[7]

For the record, Vladimir Gershuni, nephew of Grigory Gershuni (a founder
of the Socialist Revolutionary Party), was sentenced to ten years in 1949,
and became something of a prominent dissident in the 1960s, suffering
psychiatric abuse at the hands of the authorities.[8] Boris Burkovsky later
became the curator of the museum on the battleship *Avrora*, unshakeable in
his communist convictions. Lev Grossman (1920-85) wrote stories, sketches
and scripts for popular scientific films, these last including *Malen'kaia
istoriia* (*A Small Story*,1957) and *Chelovek v zelënoi perchatke* (*The Person
in the Green Glove*,1967).[9]

Through each of three key characters, a peasant, a worker and an intellectual, the reader learns much about the peasantry, the proletariat and the intelligentsia, and how, if at all, they interact. Thus, in its own way, *Ivan Denisovich*, to recall Belinsky's phrase regarding *Evgenii Onegin*, becomes an encyclopaedia of Soviet life. Fragmented characterisation allows for the assembling of a rich and rounded mosaic, but one which has drama and movement. Kodjak's assertion that *Ivan Denisovich* is a 'virtually plotless account' (p. 26) only really holds water if one has a very restricted notion of what constitutes 'plot'.

Ivan Denisovich Shukhov and the Peasant World

In some respects Solzhenitsyn displays characteristics of 'village prose', arguably the most dominant fictional form in officially sanctioned Russian literature from the late 1950s through to the mid-1980s. A one-time close friend of Solzhenitsyn was Boris Mozhaev, one of the leading exponents of the genre. Solzhenitsyn's second published story *Matryona's Home*, written at approximately the same time as *Ivan Denisovich*, is clearly in the mainstream of village prose. One of the chief characters in *The First Circle* is Spiridon, the archetypal stoic Russian peasant who appears in a chapter with the affectionately ironic title 'Going to the People'. The allusion to the nineteenth-century Populists is obvious. Stephen Carter has argued persuasively that the tradition closest to Solzhenitsyn is the 'Native Soil Movement' (*pochvennichestvo*) of the 1850s and 60s. He defines what the movement stood for as follows:

> While possessing some of the characteristics of conservative nationalists, the *pochvenniki* were also, paradoxically enough, radicals. They were opposed to the institution of serfdom, and to the bureaucratic features of the autocracy. Thus they did not equate the nation with the state, or with any particular form of state organisation. They believed that the essence of the nation, its native soil, was best understood and represented by the people (*narod*), and that national development could best take place on the basis of the peasant commune (*obshchina*). Thus nationalist and democratic feelings reinforced one another in this school of thought. However, this is not to say that they equated the nation with its people: they said merely that the people were most likely to understand their nation best, whereas the upper classes and the intelligentsia were unable to interpret correctly the true interests of Russia.[10]

On the surface, village prose seemed inimical to Soviet power, given that it often depicted with affection backward and ignorant peasants and highlighted rural deprivation. Yet it also displayed qualities which were congenial to the authorities: characters were plausible, hardworking, fiercely patriotic, morally sound and stoical in the face of adversity, whether that adversity was inspired by the natural elements, Stalin's collectivisation programme or the Nazi war machine. A degree of wishful thinking also developed in such fiction, as folk memories spoke of how well the Russian rustic had eaten and conducted himself before the dark days of Stalinism. Kathleen Parthé subtitles her comprehensive study of the genre 'The Radiant Past'.[11] All of these remarks have some bearing on Solzhenitsyn's hero.

Ivan is forever busy, if not doing something, then thinking, planning or remembering. We have a fairly full picture of him physically and a good idea of his biography. He has lost some teeth because of an attack of scurvy in Ust-Izhma in 1943 (Paris, pp. 13-14; Willetts, p. 9). Later we learn that he has lost 'half' his teeth, has a bald patch and has been treading the earth for forty years (in 1951) (Paris, p. 33; Willetts, p. 35). In any event, his head is shaved (Paris, p. 15; Willetts, p. 12), and in the sick-bay he feels the ten-day growth of his beard. On being searched on his return to the camp, he reflects that if he spends a term in the punishment cell, it will be difficult for him to get back to the 'wiry, not hungry, but not full condition' (*zhilistoe, ne golodnoe, i ne sytoe sostoianie*, p. 90; Willetts, p. 111) which he is in now. We are given a great deal more detail about his clothing: the padded trousers that he had kept on all night, with the greasy patch above the left knee with his serial number in faded black ink (Paris, p. 10; Willetts, p. 5); or his dressing for work parade: two lots of footcloths (*portianki*), the good ones on first, then his felt boots (*valenki*), his overcoat (*bushlat*) over his sleeveless coat (*telogreika*), and a piece of string (leather straps are forbidden) round his middle (Paris, pp. 22-3; Willetts, p. 21). For the march out to the building site he puts on a facecloth against the wind. Though some of the prisoners do find scope for sartorial individuality, in the main the appearance of the prisoners is uniform and dehumanising. Beneath the clothing though, each is a unique being.

Ivan has served eight years of a ten-year sentence. He comes from the village of Temgenyovo. He left home on 23 June 1941 when war broke out and has not seen his family since. Officially he is in prison for treason, having been judged to have deliberately gone over to the Germans and then come back from a POW camp to carry out a mission for the enemy. In fact, what had happened was that in February 1942 the whole of the Red Army in the North-Western sector was surrounded by the Germans, and had no supplies of either food or ammunition. The Germans captured the Red Army-men in groups, and Ivan, after a few days in their hands, was able to escape with four others. Three of them were killed by friendly Russian fire, so only Ivan and one other made it back alive. However, no one believed that they could have escaped from the Germans, so they were promptly arrested. Ivan was beaten until he signed a confession. He then spent seven years in camps in the North, three years hauling logs, often working night shifts if the daily quota was not reached (Paris, pp. 49-50; Willetts, pp. 56-8), and Ivan concludes that life in his present camp is more peaceful, even if it is a special camp. The camp which stays most clearly in his mind is Ust-Izhma: he has fashioned a spoon with 'Ust-Izhma, 1944' scratched on it, and one might surmise that this was his only previous camp were it not for the remark that this spoon had travelled all over the North with him (Paris, p. 15; Willetts, p. 12). In this camp he had earned thirty roubles a month whereas in his present camp there are no wages (Paris, p. 103; Willetts, p. 128). But in this special regime camp you can speak freely, unlike in Ust-Izhma, where if you so much as whispered that there were no matches available outside the camp you could get another 10 years (Paris, p. 105; Willetts, p. 131). Ivan never forgets his first foreman's advice about the 'law of the *taiga*' (Paris, pp. 7-8; Willetts, p. 2), whereby scroungers, malingerers and informers die first.

The most intriguing thing about these 'recent' recollections is that they are mixed, portraying an existence that has some pluses and some minuses, with the hero, on balance, preferring his present camp. When we are taken further back in time, obviously prior to collectivisation, life is depicted as unambiguously better:

> In the camps Shukhov more than once remembered how they used to eat in the village previously: potatoes – whole frying pans of them, porridge – iron pots of it, and earlier still, when there weren't the collective farms, meat in great big slices. And milk they lapped up – enough to make your belly burst.
>
> (Paris, p. 36; Willetts, pp. 39-40)

At lunch Ivan recalls how as a lad (so clearly this relates to well before the 1930s) he fed 'heaps' (*skolishcha*) of oats to horses, never dreaming that he would want, with all his soul, a handful of oats himself one day (Paris, p. 53; Willetts, p. 62). We have another snapshot of Ivan's distant former life towards the end of the wall-building scene:

> The Captain pushed the barrow up like a good gelding (*merin dobryi*).
>
> 'More,' he shouts, 'two more barrows!'
>
> By now the Captain's legs are giving way under him, but he's still hauling. Shukhov used to have a gelding like that, before there was the collective farm. Shukhov used to spare him (*ego priberegal*), but in other people's hands he turned into a living corpse (*podrezalsia on zhivo*). And they took the hide off him (*I shkuru s ego sniali*)
>
> (Paris, p. 75; Willetts, p. 90)

The idiom here is particularly rustic ('To take a hide off', or even 'two hides off' someone means 'to work a person till he drops'). Willetts' translation has for the last two sentences: 'Shukhov had taken good care of him, but when strangers got their hands on him they worked him to a frazzle. And did for him in no time.' The point about the good old days is underscored later when Ivan goes to save Tsezar a place in the queue for parcels and he recalls that when he was a free man it was easier for him to feed his whole family than it was now to feed just himself (Paris, p. 93; Willetts, p. 114).

The hero's other qualities include cunning (he has wangled his own trowel, fiddles two extra bowls of gruel at lunch, pretends that the tobacco he buys from the Latvian is not the same as before), a sensible degree of courage, as when he warns the red-haired convict not to touch other people's boots (Paris, p. 115; Willetts, p. 143), and a sense of humour, 'complaining' as he does about the shortness of the working day (Paris, p. 76; Willetts, p. 92).

However, through Ivan we gain profounder insights than these into the psychology of the peasantry. Religious issues, superstition, folk wisdom are all reflected in him and his immediate entourage. It could also be argued that there is a degree of serf mentality in him, which may temper his dignity, but more especially deals a knock-out punch to Soviet claims regarding the 'new man', social equality and the like.

While Alyoshka the Baptist is the overt religious figure in the novel and Ivan makes *prima facie* anti-religious noises, there is clearly a dimension to the hero which operates on a metaphysical plane. Mentally he equates Alyoshka with a political agitator, because he reads the Bible audibly (Paris, p. 22; Willetts, p. 20) and at lights-out the two have a full discussion on the subject of God, when Alyoshka hears Ivan thank the Lord aloud for another day being over (Paris, p. 115; Willetts, p. 144). The exchange illustrates the gulf between Russian Orthodoxy and the Baptists. The Orthodox Church underwent rehabilitation during the war, and in general, Orthodox priests were treated more leniently than some other religious groups. Baptists, by contrast, with their emphasis on content rather than form in their worship, ostensibly more concerned with religious conscience than with the pomp and outer trappings of institutionalised religion, were seen to pose more of a threat to the atheist state. Small wonder that Alyoshka is offended when Ivan tries to parry his arguments by referring to the well-heeled and licentious priest from Polomnya, and tells Ivan that the Orthodox Church has turned away from the Gospels (Paris, pp. 116-7; Willetts, pp. 145-6). When Alyoshka tells Ivan that he should be grateful for being in prison because it gives him time to think about his soul, and asks him what he needs freedom for, he is touching on a recurrent theme in Solzhenitsyn. Nerzhin, the hero of *The First Circle*, says that prison has given him time to think, and all the leading characters in that novel are freer than the guards and top officials on the outside, who are terrified of speaking their minds.

These notions are spelled with even greater force in a passage from *The Gulag Archipelago* which deals with Solzhenitsyn's conversion to Christianity. Though born into a pious family and christened in the Orthodox faith, as a young man, Solzhenitsyn, like so many of his generation, was a fervent Marxist. It was only after arrest, and nearly six years of his eight-year sentence had passed (involving rigorous, uninhibited discussions with other inmates, and an operation for cancer in February 1952), that he abandoned the Marxist faith entirely. Solzhenitsyn heads the chapter of *The Gulag Archipelago* which describes the process 'The Ascent'.

> It is *good* to think in prison, but it is not bad in camp either [...]
> And the really important thing is...that they cannot compel you
> to be a propagandist. Nor – to listen to propaganda [...]
>
> A free head – now is that not an advantage of life in the
> Archipelago?
>
> And there is one more freedom: No one can deprive you of
> your family and property – you have already been deprived of
> them.[12]

And twice, in italics, towards the end of the chapter he writes: '*Bless you, prison*' (pp. 598-9). The chapter also contains his famous poem recording his return to religion ('God of the Universe! I believe again!/Though I renounced You, You were with me!'). Solzhenitsyn also declares: 'Since then I have come to understand the truth of all the religions of the world: they struggle with the *evil inside a human being* (inside every human being). It is impossible to expel evil from the world in its entirety, but it is possible to constrict it within each person.'[13]

Ivan Denisovich does not subscribe to any religion, and Alysohka is wrong to interpret his appeals to the Almighty as indicating a latent religious strain: Ivan, no less than Nikita Khrushchev was wont to in his speeches, simply takes the Lord's name in vain – as he does when he prays that he won't be put in the punishment cells if the hacksaw blade is found (Paris, p. 90; Willetts, p. 111). Neither should Ivan's exchange with Buynovsky concerning the moon and the stars be taken as ignorance or superstition on the hero's part. The Captain is fond of explaining things to people whether they want to know or not. Ivan is feeling 'cheerful' (*veselo*, p. 78, aptly rendered by Willetts as 'playful', p. 94) when he asks him 'according to *your* science' [my italics, R.P.] where the moon disappears to, and Ivan *laughs* [my italics, R.P.] as he follows up with 'How do you know it's there, if you can't see it?' The superstition that God crumbles up the old moon to make stars, is not necessarily Ivan's, for it is prefixed with 'Round our way they used to say' (*U nas tak govorili*). When Ivan tells Buynovsky – in reply to his direct question – that when it thunders how could you not believe in God (Paris, p. 79; Willetts, p. 95), he is surely indulging in some non-committal playfulness which simultaneously discloses his awe of the natural world.

Such readiness on the part of the peasant simply to respect the natural world and establish a working relationship with it, rather than to comprehend and master it, is very much in the ethos of village prose. This at-oneness with the natural world is borne out time and again by the animal imagery throughout the text. Volkovoi lives up to his name with his wolf-like brutality; the 16-year-old Gopchik is variously likened to a piglet (Paris, p. 40; Willetts, p. 44), a calf and a squirrel (Paris, p. 45; Willetts, p. 51), a little hare (Paris, p. 51; Willetts, p. 59 has 'a little rabbit') and a goat (Paris, p. 53; Willetts, p. 62); other characters are routinely referred to as jackals, pigs, dogs or reptiles; when the column wins the race back to the camp there is 'hare's joy' (*zaiach'ia radost'*) that 'frogs are afraid even of us' (Paris, p. 87; Willetts, p. 107).

In *Ivan Denisovich* folk wisdom is ubiquitously displayed through the numerous aphorisms employed by the hero or his mind-reading creator/ narrator. Several of these have been noted already in other contexts, perhaps the most memorable being the various phrases concerning the inability of someone who is warm to understand someone who is cold: *Tëplyi ziablogo razve kogda poimët?* (Paris, p. 20; Willetts, p. 18); *Gretomu mërzlogo ne poniat'* (Paris, p. 81; Willetts, p. 98). When it is explained to the reader how the work brigade provides the discipline which forces the prisoner to apply himself diligently, there is a short aphoristic paragraph by way of introduction:

> Seems, why should a *zek* put his back into it for ten years in
> a camp? Don't want to, he'll say, and that's all there is to it.
> Drag out the day till the evening, and the night's ours.
>   (Paris, p. 43; Willetts, p. 48)

The last sentence here (in the original *Volochi den' do vechera, a noch' nasha*) is reminiscent of the adage the serfs would address to their owners: 'We're yours, but the land is ours' (*My vashi, a zemlia nasha*). Back in Ivan's village all the buildings were made of wood, but in the camp the hero is able to acquire the skills of a brick-layer: 'Anyone who can do two things with his hands, will pick up another ten' (*Kto dva dela rukami znaet, tot eshchë i desiat' podkhvatit*, p. 70; Willetts, p. 84). Tyurin's remark that the Creator does exist after all, and that 'Your patience is long, but you hit hard' (*Dolgo terpish', da bol'no b'ësh'*, p. 62; Willetts, p. 73) is similarly to be seen as a piece of folk wisdom as much as in terms of religious conviction. At supper Ivan decides to save his bread ration for the next day, since: 'The belly is a villain, doesn't remember an old good deed, it'll ask again tomorrow' (*Briukho – zlodei, starogo dobra ne pomnit, zavtra opiat' sprosit*, p. 102; Willetts, p. 127).

The import of all these sayings, culled from Dahl, or overheard or half-invented, is manifold. They certainly add local colour and enrich our impression of the hero's psychology. They are also a very effective foil to political slogans. They are also a foil to the pseudo-folk proverbs, officially propounded in Soviet times in an attempt to amalgamate home-spun philosophy with social command. As verbalised or enacted, Ivan's philosophy may seem contradictory, but its coherence resides in its being geared to the survival of his body and his dignity. He can cower or dissemble on occasion, but his victories are indisputable. There is a moral bedrock and a tragedy in his inability to understand how his village can cope without conscientious workers and in his shock that there is easy money to be had from stencilling carpets, rather than honest earnings from farming (Paris, pp. 32-3; Willetts, pp. 33-4).

Andrei Prokofievich Tyurin and the Workers' State

Many of Tyurin's personal features we dealt with in the examination of the epic qualities of *Ivan Denisovich*. However, through him, and a few other characters, notably Buynovsky and Pavlo and through certain observations, we gain an insight into the entire world of the Soviet proletariat, a world in many ways at odds with Ivan's psychology.

Solzhenitsyn himself had been a brigade leader for a time, first at the New Jerusalem labour camp some thirty miles outside Moscow in 1945. He had been a dismal failure, put in charge of a gang of common criminals who refused to work and given no means by which to discipline them. His second spell as a leader was in Ekibastuz, in the time and place that *Ivan Denisovich* is set. This time he fared much better, though he seems to have been uniquely lucky, involved more in administration and negotiating work rates than in day-to-day labour.[14] He did much better than most of the brigade leaders, when in the aftermath of a mutiny at the camp in January 1952, he found himself in negotiations on the prisoners' behalf with high-ranking officers from the Ministry of the Interior, which resulted in a temporary victory for the underdogs.

The high priority given to urbanisation and industrialisation in the Soviet state, with the proletariat, according to the propaganda at least, at the vanguard of social development, hardly bears fruit in *Ivan Denisovich*. On the contrary, things get done almost in spite of all the scientific planning, norm-setting and mathematics, rather than because of them. We are told uncompromisingly that more depends on the percentage that the gang leader can get for the job, than the job itself, and that a given piece of work needs to be shown by those who do it to be dearer than it really is (Paris, p. 44; Willetts, p. 50). The leader has to use *blat* to fix the rate (here the term denotes bribery rather than personal connections), but what is really at work here – though the word is not used – is *tukhta* (falsifying output statistics), a term that Solzhenitsyn discusses at length in *The Gulag Archipelago*.

The technology available for producing things is in a markedly sorrier state than the technology used to deprive people of their freedom (search-lights, automatic weapons, watch-towers). The electrical hoist does not work and cannot be repaired. We are told that no matter how many sites

Ivan has been on, the machinery always either broke down itself or the *zek*s have broken it themselves to get a rest (Paris, p. 73; Willetts, p. 88).

The near universal picture of waste and inefficiency is best exemplified by the laborious roll-calls, at the start of the work parade, at the end of the shift, on re-entering the camp, and the two at lights-out. The prisoners are up at five o'clock in the morning, but no real work begins for Ivan's gang until after lunch. At the evening roll-call Ivan reflects that an illiterate herdsman would know effortlessly if all his calves were there, but that the guards, who are supposed to be trained (*a etikh i nataskivaiut*), have trouble totting up their charges (Paris, p. 114; Willetts, pp. 142-3).

Poor technology and time-consuming procedures are only two brakes on efficiency. On top of these are the layers of bureaucracy. Continuing the passage about the percentages being more important than the job itself, we have:

> And figure it out – who are all these percentages for? For the camp. The camp rakes in thousands extra from the construction site and awards its lieutenants bonuses. To that Volkovoi for that whip of his. And you'll get two hundred grammes of bread extra in the evening. Two hundred grammes rules your life. The White Sea canal was built on two hundred grammes.
>
> (Paris, pp. 44-5; Willetts, p. 50)

The Gulag Archipelago devotes many pages to the appalling conditions under which convict labourers operated to complete the White Sea canal show-case project, a project which turned out, in the author's view, to be a white elephant, a victim of *tukhta* and as such too shallow to take heavy shipping.

The notion of massive over-manning at the top, of institutionalised parasitism, is nowhere better illustrated than in the case of the camp's catering arrangements, especially at the building site:

> A couple of people manned the kitchen – the cook and the hygienist. In the morning, when they were to come out of the camp, the cook gets the groats in the big kitchen in the camp. Maybe about fifty grammes for each lad, a kilo for the brigade, a bit less than a *pood* for all the site. The cook himself is not going to carry that sack of groats three kilo-meters, so he gets a stooge (*shestërka*) to do it. Rather than breaking your own back, it's better to dish out an extra portion to that stooge at the workers' (*rabotiagi*) expense. Bringing the water, the firewood, lighting the stove – the cook doesn't do that himself, workers and goners (*dokhodi-agi*) again – they all get a portion each, don't begrudge what ain't yours. Also, you were supposed to eat your food

without leaving the mess-hall: the bowls had to be taken out of the camp (you couldn't leave them at the site, the free workers would nick them overnight), so they took fifty of them out, no more, and they were washed up there and turned round sharpish (the bowl carrier also got a portion over the top). So as to stop them taking bowls out of the mess-hall they put another stooge on the door – to stop the bowls going out. But no matter how he kept a look-out – all the same they would still take them off, people still talked him round or distracted his attention. So they had to let a collector go all round the whole site: to collect the dirty bowls and cart them back to the kitchen. And one portion goes to this man. And another to the other one.

(Paris, pp. 51-2; Willetts, pp. 59-60)

A third lengthy paragraph describes the minimal duties performed by the cook, the hygienist and the duty foreman, who all fill their own stomachs at the expense of the prisoners. Towards the end of the book we see again the corruption and power involved in the distribution of food, with the manager of the mess-hall and his *zek* assistant, nicknamed 'the lame one', well-fed themselves and able to hold the convicts at bay outside the hall. The manager holds thousands of lives in his hands and once when the convicts tried to beat him up, the cooks (with a strong implication that these are all common criminals) sprang to his defence (Paris, p. 97; Willetts, p. 120).

We see almost nothing of the 'work' that is undertaken by those involved in planning and norm-setting. When Ivan takes Tsezar's lunch to him, we have primarily the memorable discussion about Eisenstein, though this is preceded by a near-unattributed diatribe (probably from the site manager) about too much being spent on wages, and too many materials being used, and the prisoners wasting timber and cement. Two accountants, also prisoners, are toasting bread, having made a griddle out of barbed wire (Paris, p. 59; Willetts, p. 69) – so the misappropriation of goods seems to stop nowhere. And one detects a mental sneer in Ivan at Shkuropatenko, who will not be seeing his tar-paper again (Paris, p. 59; Willetts, p. 69). The office is overheated and 'if you sat down for a moment, you'd fall asleep right away' (Paris, p. 58; Willetts, p. 68). In the confrontation between Tyurin and Der, the latter is called an 'infection' (*zaraza*, 'shit' in Willetts) and a 'blood-sucker' (*krovosos*) (Paris, p. 71; Willetts, p. 85), quite common terms of abuse in Russian, but singularly apt here. Whilst there is some poetic justice in the fact that Fetyukov was once a well-placed bureaucrat and is now a camp scavenger whose self-abasement is limitless, of equal importance is that he is forever a parasite, no matter what his social standing, just another burden for the real workers to bear.

It is in the nature of things that we learn very little about the free workers,

but we can draw conclusions. If they are inclined to steal bowls from the
prisoners, one suspects that they are not so well off themselves. Yet
occasionally the prisoners get information from them (as Ivan does about
the temperature forecast). The reader is led to further supposition, given the
subsequent intriguing detail:

> Something could be heard a great way off: somewhere a
> tractor was roaring in the housing estate, while by the side
> of the main road an excavator kept screeching. And every
> pair of felt boots, wherever in the camp anyone was walking
> along or dashing over somewhere – made a scraping noise.
> And there was no wind.   (Paris, p. 103; Willetts, p. 128)

This scene is consonant with the more relaxed tempo of the day as it draws
to a close. Yet the sounds outside the camp imply that at least some free
workers are still hard at it, and the noise they make contrasts with the
subdued footfalls of the *zeks*. With no wind, perhaps the reader is being
given a quiet opportunity to reflect, as Solzhenitsyn himself had as a
prisoner, and to contemplate how much more productive the workers' state
could be if it were free...

Against such a picture of rampant inefficiency and mismanagement, we
have the resourcefulness of Ivan and his ilk, and the epic and classically
heroic qualities of Tyurin and his kind. On a purely socio-economic level
Ivan Denisovich can be construed as an illustration of the well-attested
contention that in the long run slave labour is simply unproductive and
wastes talents. Nicholas I said that serfdom was the reason Russia had no
trade or industry. Khrushchev was to learn a similar lesson.

Tsezar Markovich and the Intelligentsia

> Over the years I have had much occasion to ponder this word,
> the *intelligentsia*. We are all very fond of including ourselves
> in it – but you see not all of us belong. In the Soviet Union
> this word has acquired a completely distorted meaning. They
> began to classify among the intelligentsia all those who don't
> work (and are afraid to) with their hands. All the Party,
> government, military, and trade-union bureaucrats have been
> included [...]
>   And yet the truth is that not one of these criteria permits a
> person to be classified in the intelligentsia. [...] The intellec-
> tual is not defined by professional pursuit and type of occu-
> pation. Nor are good upbringing and good family enough in
> themselves to produce an intellectual. An intellectual is a
> person whose interests in and preoccupation with the
> spiritual side of life are insistent and constant and not forced

by external circumstances, even flying in the face of them.
An intellectual is a person whose thought is nonimitative.[15]

In this abbreviated extract from *The Gulag Archipelago* we see that
Solzhenitsyn's views on the Russian intelligentsia indeed do hark back to
pre-Revolutionary times and are at odds with the Soviet concept of the
intelligentsia as no more than a highly trained élite.

It is an extraordinary tribute to Solzhenitsyn's powers of observation
that, though himself an intellectual who consorted primarily with other
intellectuals while in confinement, he succeeded so completely in penetrat-
ing the mind of a peasant. Yet, how does the peasant view the social group
from which his creator comes?

Ivan Denisovich knows the working class and the peasantry inside out,
their strengths and weaknesses. He can admire, and aspire to, the very best
qualities in them, even to the extent of showing leadership and initiative.
Faced with the intelligentsia though, he is on the whole indifferent, passive
and uncomprehending, and the attitudes are mutual. It is here that we see the
biggest failure of the Soviet system – to create a classless society, to bring
about the much vaunted *rapprochement* between town and country. It is
here, too, that one detects Solzhenitsyn's own discomfort with his own class.

Ivan's first encounter with the intelligentsia comes in the sick-bay where
the 'medical orderly' (*fel'dsher*), Vdovushkin, who is in fact an ex-student
of literature, takes his temperature. Ivan's discomfiture is reflected in his
uncertain mode of address: first he addresses the orderly by his name and
patronymic, but a moment later by the diminutive of his first name, a rapid
transition from respectful formality to familiarity (Paris, p. 18; Willetts, p. 15).
Ivan has no occasion to use either the familiar *ty* (thou) or the more formal
vy; perhaps he deliberately avoids them so as not to commit an indiscretion.
Yet the young prisoner, who by virtue of his education, albeit interrupted,
has landed a cushy job, adopts an unequivocally patronising *ty* to talk back
to the hero. Such is his nonchalance that he eventually provokes the thought
in the hero that a warm man cannot understand a cold one.

Ivan is a fish out of water in the sick-bay, utterly fazed by the whiteness
of everything and the tranquillity. The way in which he observes Vdovushkin
writing poetry ('Everso even lines, each one starting neatly beneath another
one with a capital letter', Paris, p. 18; Willetts, p. 15) is a fine example of
the Tolstoyan device of 'making it strange'. Ivan neither knows nor cares
whether this is poetry, but he is right that it is nothing to do with him or with
the orderly's duties. The new doctor, Stepan Grigorich, (whom we never
see – all the doctors' doors are closed as they are still sleeping) is a good
example of the Soviet 'intelligentsia' Solzhenitsyn is so dismissive of: he
is all 'hustle and bustle' (*gonkii takoi da zvonkii*, p. 19; Willetts, p. 17) and
takes the line that work (gardening and the like) is the best cure for sick convicts. Ivan reflects that horses die of work. Yet at the same time the doctor can

fix up the literature student as an orderly so that he will get the chance to write in prison the things that he is not allowed to write outside (Paris, p. 20; Willetts, p. 17). The 'them and us' attitude is reinforced with the mention of the 'ignorant' workers to whom Vdovushkin learns to administer intravenous injections. Literally the adjective *tëmnyi* could be translated as 'dark', and it carries connotations of the pre-revolutionary 'ignorant common folk' (*tëmnyi narod*), which in theory contrasted with the new enlightened collective farm workers of the Soviet era. Having sketched the Soviet intelligentsia in this way, Solzhenitsyn then proceeds to a more complex, and arguably more sympathetic, picture of an *intelligent*. Tsezar Markovich, as noted earlier, is based on Lev Grossman, who by an extraordinary coincidence was a pupil of Valentin Turkin, a script-writer and cinema expert who had a Chair at the Moscow Institute of Cinematography, of which he was a founder. Turkin was also an uncle of Natalya Reshetovskaya, Solzhenitsyn's first wife, whom the couple got to know well just before the war.[16]

> In Tsezar were mixed all nations: either Greek, or Jew, or gipsy – you couldn't tell which. Still young. Used to make films for the cinema. But he hadn't finished the first one even before they put him in prison. He had a black, walrus moustache, thick.   (Paris, p. 25; Willetts, p. 24)

Persistently aloof, he usually smokes a pipe so that others will not pester him for a smoke, begrudging not the tobacco but his interrupted thoughts. 'He smoked in order to awaken strong thought in himself and allow it to find something' (Paris, p. 25; Willetts, p. 24). However, on this first occasion he is smoking a cigarette and both Fetyukov and Ivan are hoping to finish it. There is significance in the fact that he gives the cigarette end to Ivan, not to the scavenger, and indeed there is an unstated rapport between the hero and the intellectual, despite the much commented on scene where Ivan takes him his lunch. Ivan forever performs services for Tsezar and always receives payment of one kind or another. He saves him a place in the parcel queue, he lends him a knife (possession of which could cost the owner ten days in the cells), he protects Tsezar's food parcel for him during the evening roll-calls. Hardly mutated at all, the relationship is that of the loyal and *well-treated* domestic serf to that of his master, as one witnesses just occasionally in Tolstoy and Turgenev. Tsezar's sense of patronage complements Ivan's practicality. Neither of them sees any reason to understand the other on an intellectual plane.

Thus, when Tsezar does not even notice Ivan handing him his lunch, so absorbed is he in his discussion about Eisenstein, it only marginally reflects, it might be argued, on the intellectual morally – on numerous other occasions he does take notice of Ivan and rewards him accordingly. More dubious is the *content* of Tsezar's remarks to Kh-123. Solzhenitsyn's regard for the Orthodox Church notwithstanding, the too rarefied and precious tone is set by Tsezar's pipe, the smoke from which is like 'incense in church' (Paris, p. 58; Willetts, p. 68). When Tsezar says that objectively Eisenstein is a genius, his interlocutor responds that there is so much art in *Ivan The Terrible* that it is not art at all and is a most disgusting justification for tyranny (Paris, p. 59; Willetts, p. 69). We need only recall Solzhenitsyn's own view, set out most explicitly in his Nobel Prize address, that art and literature should have a moral and utilitarian function and should convey 'the truth', to conclude that Solzhenitsyn is more on the side of Kh-123, though he relishes the intellectual fray. Indeed, there is an affectionate mockery in the portrayal of Tsezar: at the end of the heroic shift, which has done so much to raise human dignity but at the expense of physical exertion, he is now trying to convince Buynovsky of his ideas on Eisenstein, this time with reference to *Battleship Potëmkin*. The captain, who after all knows more about the navy than Tsezar, rather implies that the mutinous sailors were better off then than the *zeks* are now: 'If they brought that meat into the camp for us instead of the shitty fish we get ...' (Paris, p. 82; Willetts, p. 100). Tsezar's regular food parcels and his fine fur hat, which, probably through bribery, he has been given permission to wear (Paris, p. 94; Willetts, p. 116) add to his slightly ridiculous aspect. Given Solzhenitsyn's own marginally enhanced status in Ekibastuz, one might also detect an element of self-reference on the author's part.

Such a view is supported by the encounter between Tsezar and Pyotr Mikhalych, 'an eccentric wearing glasses' (*chudak v ochkakh*, p. 94; Willetts, pp. 116-7) in the parcel queue. The latter refers to a 'most interesting review of Zavadsky's première' in the newspaper he has just received. Yuri Zavadsky, actor and theatre manager, former director of the Red Army Theatre in Moscow, was relegated to Rostov in 1936, having been excessively innovative in the capital. The young Solzhenitsyn, harbouring ambitions for a theatrical career at the time, had attended his drama classes. (Their paths nearly crossed again, in 1963, when Tvardovsky suggested to Solzhenitsyn that Zavadsky, by now an old friend of the *Novy mir* editor and head of the Mossovet Theatre, stage Solzhenitsyn's play *The Lovegirl and the Innocent* [also known as *The Tenderfoot and the Tramp*].)[17]

Ivan's disparaging view of the two intellectuals in the parcel queue elaborates on the mental gulf between peasant and intellectual:

> These Muscovites sniff each other out a mile off, like dogs.
> And, when they get together, they keep on sniffing round
> each other, keep on sniffing in their own way. And they
> gabble on nineteen to the dozen to see who can get the most
> words in (*lopochut bystro-bystro, kto bol'she slov skazhet*).
> And when they gabble on like that, hardly any Russian words
> crop up, listening to them is just like listening to Latvians or
> Romanians.   (Paris, p. 94; Willetts, p. 117)

Onc of the real achievements of *Ivan Denisovich* is that while displaying
with such authenticity the various social groups that make up Soviet society
and the gaps between them, it also, and with equal credibility, portrays the
common humanity that can also obtain, irrespective of social grouping. A
conformist Soviet critic could pass this off as a form of *splochënnost'*, class
solidarity. Yet a more precise definition of it might be found in passages in
Solzhenitsyn's *Cancer Ward*, where Shulubin alludes to Kropotkin's *Mutual
Aid* and advocates, rather piously, one might argue, 'ethical socialism'.

Two factors emerge from *Ivan Denisovich*'s social anatomy. Firstly, there
is a good deal of sympathetic interaction, on the emotional, if not on the verbal,
level between the social groups. There is some bonding between Buynovsky
and Tsezar, between both of them and Ivan, between Ivan and Tyurin, between
Alyoshka and Ivan. Circumstance has made the peasant Ivan into a worker, a
sea captain into a worker, turned a Red Army-man into a foreman, a script writer
into a production planner, a literature student into a medic, a well-placed
bureaucrat into a scavenger. Nearly all of these, with the possible exception of
Fetyukov, have some degree of power. For some of them that power rests on
authority, the authority which each character establishes for himself.

So, secondly, an alternative hierarchy emerges, quite independent of the
official power structures, but contingent on each individual's ability to
confront the classical epic notion of his lot, his *moira*, from one day to the
next. This may result in a re-emergence of the social relations of a former
era (as in the case of Tsezar and Ivan), but the burden of the text is that these
would seem preferable, both morally and in the interests of economic
efficiency, to those created by Soviet power. It could be added that this
hierarchy also depends on the ability of the individual to preserve at least
some residual sense of dignity and decency, to distinguish for himself, quite
independently of any ideology or institutionalised religion, between good
and evil. Here we are brought back to the importance of individual conscience (*sovest'*) in Solzhenitsyn's moral investigations.

Ivan's triumph resides in his ability to establish his legitimate place in
the alternative hierarchy, a hierarchy which, unlike the Soviet variety, makes
no bland and hypocritical claims to equality and freedom.

Ivan tries not to count the days to the end of his sentence, and knows that
there is always a possibility that he will simply be given a second term (Paris,
p. 33, pp. 48-9; Willetts, p. 35, pp. 55-6). The closing words of the novel denote
not just the scale of the Stalinist nightmare, but also Ivan Denisovich's
continuing ability, in or out of prison, to retain his identity as a human being,
with all its contradictions. In this, as in so many of Solzhenitsyn's works,
there is, despite their bitter subject matter, affirmation and even optimism.

Notes to Part Two

Chapter I (pp. 57-66)

1. Solzhenitsyn, A., *The Gulag Archipelago 2, 1918-1956, Parts II-IV*, translated by Thomas Whitney, London, 1975, pp. 181-2. The corresponding passage in the original is *Sobranie sochinenii*, vol. 6, pp. 178-9.

2. Scammell, pp. 557-8.

3. Bradbury, M. and McFarlane, J. (eds.), *Modernism 1890-1930*, Sussex, U.K. and New Jersey, 1978, p. 32.

4. Ibid., p. 26.

5. Ibid.

6. Ibid., p. 27.

7. Kafka, F., *The Trial*, translated by Willa and Edwin Muir, first published in London, 1935. This reprint, Harmondsworth, 1984, p. 7.

8. Heller, E., *Kafka*, London, 1974, pp. 81-2.

9. Page references to *Ivan Denisovich* will be inserted into the text henceforth, firstly relating to the authorised (Paris) Collected Works *Sobranie sochinenii*, vol. 3, pp. 7-122, and then to the Willetts translation, thus, as here: (Paris, p. 7; Willetts, p. 1). Unless otherwise indicated the translations used in my discussion are my own, and they are very much working versions, veering towards the literal, and designed to give the uninitiated an inkling of the Russian or to emphasise a particular point.

10. Cornwell, N., *James Joyce and the Russians*, London, 1992, p. 13.

11. Bullock, A., 'The Double Image', in Bradbury, M. and McFarlane, J., *op. cit.*, p. 58.

12. Ibid.

13. Ibid., p. 62.

Chapter II (pp. 67-81)

1. Feuer, K., 'Solzhenitsyn and the Legacy of Tolstoy', in Dunlop, J., Haugh, R., Klimoff, A. (eds.), *Aleksandr Solzhenitsyn: Critical Essays and Documentary Materials*, Second Edition, 1975, pp. 129-146.

2. Scammell, p. 421.

3. Scammell, p. 52.

4. Pasternak, B., 'Three Letters', in *Encounter*, August 1960, p. 5.

5. For an interesting discussion of the way Solzhenitsyn has been billed as a Socialist Realist by those wishing to denigrate him, as well as by those Soviet worthies who initially championed him, and the depiction of the work ethic see Nicholson, M., 'Solzhenitsyn as "Socialist Realist"' in *In the Party Spirit: Socialist Realism and Literary Practice in the Soviet Union, East Germany and China*, Chung, H. et al (eds.), Rodopi, Amsterdam, 1996, pp. 55-68.

6. *Gulag*, translated by Thomas Whitney, vol. 1, p. 13, Footnote. The corresponding Russian passage is to be found in *Arkhipelag GULag*, vol. 1, Paris, 1973, p. 27. Interestingly, the Collected Works omit most of this passage (see *Sobranie sochinenii*, vol. 5, p. 24). Presumably the author, now in exile and even keener to draw the West's attention to the evils of the Soviet *government*, felt that the Russian *people* should not be held even partially responsible for its own enslavement.

Chapter III (pp. 82-98)

1. See, for example, *Tolstoy: The Comprehensive Vision* by E.B. Greenwood, London, 1975; 'Tolstoy and the Development of Realism', in *Studies in European Realism* by Georgi Lukács, reprinted London, 1972, pp. 126-205. The term 'totality of objects' (p. 151) Lukács borrows from Hegel; see also remarks in *Tolstoy and the Novel* by John Bayley, London, 1966.

2. Christian, R.F., *Tolstoy: A Critical Introduction*, Cambridge, 1969, p. 107.

3. Kodjak, A., *Alexander Solzhenitsyn*, Boston, 1978, p. 27.

4. Ibid., p. 28.

5. Moody, C., *Solzhenitsyn*, Second Revised Edition, Edinburgh, 1976, p. 38.

6. Labedz, L. (ed.), *Solzhenitsyn: A Documentary Record*, second Revised Edition, Harmondsworth, 1974, pp. 48-9; see also Scammell, pp. 483-6.

7. Scammell, pp. 384-5.

8. See Rubenstein, J., *Soviet Dissidents: Their Struggle for Human Rights*, Beacon Press, Boston, 1980, p. 139, p. 229 and p. 231; and Bloch, S. and Reddaway, P., *Russia's Political Hospitals: The Abuse of Psychiatry in the Soviet Union*, Victor Gollancz, London, 1977, *passim*.

9. Grossman's obituary appeared in *Vecherniaia Moskva*, December 13, 1985, p. 4.

10. Carter, S., *The Politics of Solzhenitsyn*, London, 1977, p. 142.

11. Parthé, K. , *Russian Village Prose: The Radiant Past*, Princeton, 1992.

12. *Gulag*, vol. 2, translated by Thomas Whitney, p. 589. The corresponding passage in the Russian original (Paris) edition is *Sobranie sochinenii*, vol. 6, 'Arkhipelag Gulag II-IV', pp. 562-3.

13. Ibid., p. 597. The corresponding passage in the Russian original (Paris) edition is as above, p. 570.

14. Scammell, pp. 286-7.

15. *Gulag*, translated by Thomas Whitney, vol. 2, pp. 266-7. The corresponding passage in the Russian (Paris) original is *Sobranie sochinenii*, vol. 6, pp. 258-9.

16. Scammell, pp. 103-4.

17. Scammell, p. 80, p. 455. Incidentally, it seems likely that the review referred to is that in *Vecherniaia Moskva,* 9 December 1950, of Zavadsky's production of *Rassvet nad Moskvoi*.

Afterword

After his brief honeymoon with the Soviet establishment, Solzhenitsyn was totally proscribed, then vilified, expelled from the Writers' Union in 1969, harassed, eventually arrested and physically ejected from the Soviet Union in 1974. The only other Soviet citizen to have suffered this last indignity had been Leon Trotsky, and later, of course, he was assassinated by a Stalinist agent. In the Soviet press Solzhenitsyn was called a traitor and blasphemer, while his fellow laureate, Mikhail Sholokhov, addressing a Congress of collective farm workers, drew an unmistakable parallel between him and a Colorado beetle.[1] When Solzhenitsyn was awarded the Nobel Prize for Literature in 1970, the Soviet Government denounced the Nobel Committee for its political meddling and cold war machinations, and it was made clear that should the writer travel to Stockholm to receive this highest of honours, he would not be allowed to return.

It is therefore all the more gratifying that the author of *One Day in the Life of Ivan Denisovich* should at last be accorded in his homeland his proper place in Russian letters. Books with titles such as *From Gorky to Solzhenitsyn* and *From Blok to Solzhenitsyn* (see Bibliography) illustrate how times have changed. Solzhenitsyn's first published work still retains its cherished place within the author's *oeuvre*, and it has been reissued many times in the last few years. Critical works on Solzhenitsyn rightly pay close attention to it. Some Russians in informal discussions will argue, not uncontentiously it could be said, that it is the best book he has ever written.

Throughout his career Solzhenitsyn has been destined to be used as a political football whatever the social and political context in which he finds himself. In a very recent book by Vladimir Bondarenko, devoted to the 'twenty best writers in Russia', we are informed that 'The main thing about Solzhenitsyn's art is its deeply national Russian prose'.[2] For many other readers, however, Solzhenitsyn will be most important for his commitment to 'truth', as he sees it.

His detractors might argue that his achievement has been exaggerated, that he was lucky, because he was simply 'the first' to publish – to be allowed to publish – on the theme of the labour camps. It is, of course, the case that there is now a very large body of writing (fiction, poetry, memoirs) about the camps, and Solzhenitsyn's contribution is just one of many. It is therefore fitting that critics should go in for some comparisons. This is what

V. Chalmaev does when writing about *Ivan Denisovich* in his 'life and works' study, making repeated references to arguably the other greatest 'prison camp' prose writer of the Soviet era, Varlam Shalamov.

Perhaps, given the never-ending arguments about Solzhenitsyn, we should leave the last word to Chalmaev:

> Ivan Denisovich Shukhov has created his own world, having dropped out of the generally accepted system of 'for' and 'against', out of the ritual of voting and discussions [...] The whole famous scene of the wall-building is one of the pinnacles of Solzhenitsyn's art [...] One might say, if one were not to take fright at the banality of the rhetoric, that the whole scene is a hymn, a song, a prayer to freedom.[3]

Notes

1. Sholokhov, M., 'Schast'e zhit' sredi takogo velikolepnogo naroda', *Literaturnaia gazeta*, 3 December, 1969.

2. Bondarenko, V., 'Sterzhnevaia slovesnost' Aleksandra Solzhenitsyna', in *Real'naia literatura: Dvadtsat' luchshikh pisatelei Rossii*, Paleia, Moscow, 1996, p. 37.

3. Chalmaev, V., *Aleksandr Solzhenitsyn: Zhizn' i tvorchestvo*, Prosveshchenie, Moscow, 1994, pp. 59-60 and p. 67.

Selected Bibliography

Soviet Russian Texts of *One Day in the Life of Ivan Denisovich*

Odin den' Ivana Denisovicha in *Novyi mir*, no. 11, 1962, pp. 8-74.
Odin den' Ivana Denisovicha, (Roman-Gazeta no. 1), 1963.
Odin den' Ivana Denisovicha, Sovetskii pisatel', 1963.

Some Russian-language Western Texts of *One Day in the Life of Ivan Denisovich*

Odin den' Ivana Denisovicha in *Sochineniia*, Possev, Frankfurt, 1964, reprinted 1968, pp. 5-133.
Odin den' Ivana Denisovicha in *Sobranie sochinenii*, Possev, Frankfurt, 1969-70, vol. 1, pp. 5-133.
Odin den' Ivana Denisovicha, *Matrënin dvor*, YMCA-Press, Paris, 1973, pp. 9-121 (the authorised text).
Odin den' Ivana Denisovicha in *Rasskazy*, Possev, Frankfurt, 1976, pp. 5-143.
Odin den' Ivana Denisovicha, in *Sobranie sochinenii*, YMCA-Press, Paris, 1978-, vol. 3 (*rasskazy*), pp. 7-122 (the authorised text).

Since the advent of *glasnost* the story has been repeatedly published and anthologised in Russia. Note in particular:
Odin den' Ivana Denisovicha in *Rasskazy*, Sovremennik, Moscow, 1990, pp. 3-111.
Odin den' Ivana Denisovicha i drugie rasskazy, Knizhnoe izdatel'stvo, Tomsk, 1990.
Odin den' Ivana Denisovicha in *Izbrannaia proza*, Sovremennaia Rossiia, Moscow, 1990.
Odin den' Ivana Denisovicha in *Ne stoit selo bez pravednika*, Knizhnaia palata, Moscow, 1990.
Odin den' Ivana Denisovicha in *Rasskazy*, Tsentr 'Novyi mir', Moscow, 1990 (the Vermont-Paris, YMCA text).

English Translations

One Day in the Life of Ivan Denisovich, translated by Max Hayward and Ronald Hingley, Frederick Praeger, New York, 1963; reprinted as a Bantam Paperback, 1969.

One Day in the Life of Ivan Denisovich, translated by Ralph Parker, Dutton, New York and Gollancz, London, 1963; as a Penguin Paperback, 1963, numerous reprintings. A variant of this translation appeared in *Soviet Literature*, Moscow, February 1963.

One Day in the Life of Ivan Denisovich, translated by Thomas Whitney, Fawsett (Crest Paperback), New York, 1963.

One Day in the Life of Ivan Denisovich, translated by Bela Von Block, Lancer, New York, 1963, and as a Lodestone Paperback, 1973.

One Day in the Life of Ivan Denisovich, translated by Gillon Aitken, The Bodley Head, London, 1970; Revised edition, Farrar, Straus and Giroux, New York, 1971.

One Day in the Life of Ivan Denisovich, translated by Harry Willetts, with a Foreword by Alexis Klimoff, Harvill, London, 1991, and Harper-Collins Publishers and Farrar, Straus and Giroux, New York, 1991 (the authorised translation).

Criticism and Background Material

There are hundreds of books and articles on Solzhenitsyn and many of these contain comment on *One Day in the Life of Ivan Denisovich*. The following are some of the more salient items and most useful research tools:

General

By far and away the most detailed and authoritative biography is *Solzhenitsyn: A Biography*, by Michael Scammell, Hutchinson, London, 1985. The other generally available biography should be treated with caution: David Burg and George Feifer, *Solzhenitsyn*, Hodder and Stoughton, London, 1972. A sensible, if slight and now outdated, 'Life and Works' is Christopher Moody, *Solzhenitsyn*, Oliver and Boyd, Edinburgh, first published 1973, second revised edition 1976 (also listed below). Similarly, of value is Giovanni Grazzini, *Solzhenitsyn*, translated by Eric Mosbacher, Michael Joseph, London, 1973.

An excellent compilation, which itself contains a great deal of critical comment and bibliographical material, is John Dunlop, Richard Haugh, Alexis Klimoff (eds.), *Aleksandr Solzhenitsyn: Critical Essays and Documentary Materials*, Nordland, New York, 1973, second revised edition 1975.

A similar compilation relating more to Solzhenitsyn's later works, but containing some useful material germane to our discussion, is John Dunlop, Richard Haugh and Michael Nicholson, *Solzhenitsyn in Exile: Critical Essays and Documentary Materials*, Hoover Press Publications, Stanford, 1985.

Also of great interest is Leopold Labedz, *Solzhenitsyn: A Documentary Record*, second edition, Penguin, Harmondsworth, 1974.

The best bibliographical orientation, as far as the early Solzhenitsyn is concerned and *One Day in the Life of Ivan Denisovich*, is Donald Fiene,

Alexander Solzhenitsyn: An International Bibliography of Writings By and About Him, 1962-1973, Ardis, Ann Arbor, 1973.

A very full recent bibliography of works by and about Solzhenitsyn published in Russia since the advent of *glasnost* is *Aleksandr Solzhenitsyn: Bibliograficheskii ukazatel': Avgust 1988-1990*, by N.G. Levitskaia, Sovetskii fond kul'tury: Dom Mariny Tsvetaevoi, Moscow, 1991.

Of the many items published recently in Russia which deal directly with or at least touch on Solzhenitsyn we should note in particular:

Akimov, V., *Ot Bloka do Solzhenitsyna: Sud'by russkoi literatury xx veka*, Gosudarstvennaia akademiia kul'tury, Sankt-Peterburg, 1994, especially pages 34-36, 90-94, 136-138.

Bondarenko, V., 'Sterzhnevaia slovesnost' Aleksandra Solzhenitsyna', in *Real'naia literatura: Dvadtsat' luchshikh pisatelei Rossii*, Paleia, Moscow, 1996, pp. 37-60.

Chalmaev, V.A., *Aleksandr Solzhenitsyn: Zhizn' i tvorchestvo*, Prosveshchenie, Moscow, 1994.

————'Aleksandr Isaevich Solzhenitsyn', in *Russkaia literatura xx veka: chast' II: Ocherki. Portrety. Esse,* Prosveshchenie, Moscow, 1994, pp. 258-276, especially pages 264-267.

Lakshin, V., *Novyi mir vo vremena Khrushchëva: Dnevnik i poputnoe (1953-1964)*, Knizhnaia palata, Moscow, 1991.

Meshkov, Iu. A., *Aleksandr Solzhenitsyn: Lichnost', tvorchestvo, vremia*, Diamant, Ekaterinburg, 1993, especially pages 36-48.

Reshetovskaia, N., *Aleksandr Solzhenitsyn i chitaiushchaia Rossiia*, Sovetskaia Rossiia, Moscow, 1990.

Shneiberg, L., and Kondrakov, I., *Ot Gor'kogo do Solzhenitsyna*, Vysshaia shkola, Moscow, 1995, pp. 485-511.

Items in the Soviet Press

Artamonov, S., 'O povesti Solzhenitsyna', *Uchënye zapiski Literaturnogo instituta imeni Gor'kogo*, no. 2, 1963, pp. 51-61.

Baklanov, G., 'Chtob eto nikogda ne povtorilos'', *Literaturnaia gazeta*, November 22, 1962.

Broido, E., 'Takomu bol'she nikogda ne byvat'', *Poliarnaia pravda*, December 2, 1962.

Bukin, V., 'Chitaia Solzhenitsyna', *Nauka i religiia*, no. 5, 1963, pp. 90-1.

Bushin, V., 'Nasushchnyi khleb pravdy', *Neva*, no.3, 1963, pp. 180-5.

Chicherov, I., 'Vo imia budushchego', *Moskovskaia pravda*, December 8, 1962. Essays by N. Maslin and A. Khvatov on *One Day in the Life of Ivan Denisovich*, pp. 171-2 and pp. 299-302.

Drutse, I., 'O muzhestve i dostoinstve cheloveka', *Druzhba narodov*, no. 1, 1963, pp. 272-4.

Dymshits, A., 'Zhiv chelovek', *Literatura i zhizn'*, November 28, 1962.

Ermilov, V., 'Vo imia pravdy, vo imia zhizni', *Pravda*, November 23, 1962.

Fomenko, L., 'Bol'shie ozhidaniia', *Literaturnaia Rossia*, January 11, 1963.

Gubko, N., 'Chelovek pobezhdaet', *Zvezda*, no. 3, 1963, pp. 213-5.

——(ed.) *Geroi sovremennoi literatury: Stat'i*, Moscow/Leningrad, 1963. Contains Kariakin, Iu., 'Epizod iz sovremennoi bor'by idei', *Novyi mir*, no. 9, 1964, pp. 231-9.

Kashnitskii, I., 'Odin den' Ivana Denisovicha', *Sovetskaia Litva*, November 30, 1962.

Kruzhkov, N., 'Tak bylo, tak ne budet', *Ogonëk*, no. 49, 1962, pp. 28-9.

Kuznetsov, F., 'Den', ravnyi zhizni', *Znamia*, no. 1, 1963, pp. 217-221.

Kuznetsov, M., 'Chelovechnost'!', *V mire knig*, no. 1, 1963, pp. 26-7.

Lakshin, V., 'Ivan Denisovich, ego druz'ia i nedrugi', *Novyi mir*, no. 1, 1964, pp. 223-45.

Litvinov, V., 'Da budet polnoi pravda', *Trud*, December 8, 1962.

Lomidze, G., 'Neskol'ko myslei', *Literaturnaia Rossiia*, January 18, 1963. Ovcharenko, A., 'Zhizneutverdaiushchaia sila sotsialisticheskogo realizma', *Druzhba narodov*, no. 11, 1963, pp. 247-9.

Sergovantsev, N., 'Tragediia odinochestva i "sploshnoi byt"', *Oktiabr'*, no. 4, 1963, pp.198-207.

Simonov, K., 'O proshlom vo imia budushchego', *Izvestiia*, November 18, 1962.

Skul'skii, G., 'Vsia pravda', *Sovetskaia Estonia*, December 1, 1962.

Tvardovskii, A. 'Vmesto predisloviia', *Novyi mir*, no. 11, 1962, pp. 8-9.

Vinokur, T., 'O iazyke i stile povesti A. I. Solzhenitsyna "Odin den' Ivana Denisovicha"', *Voprosy kul'tury rechi*, no. 6, 1965, pp. 16-32.

The nomination of *One Day in the Life of Ivan Denisovich* for the Lenin Prize for Literature for 1964 rekindled discussion of the work. Note the following:

'V komitete po leninskim premiiam...' (announcement of the work's nomination for the Prize), *Literaturnaia gazeta*, December 28, 1963.

'Vzyskatel'nost'' (report on Lenin Prize discussions, including comment by V. Kaverin and L. Kopelev), *Literaturnaia gazeta*, February 8, 1964.

'Ot komiteta po leninskim premiiam...' (announcement short-listing *One Day in the Life of Ivan Denisovich*), *Pravda*, February 19, 1964.

'Otvetstvennost'' (report of discussions on *One Day in the Life of Ivan Denisovich*), *Literaturnaia Rossiia*, March 6, 1964.

Letters on *One Day in the Life of Ivan Denisovich* and the Lenin Prize, *Literaturnaia Rossiia*, March 27, 1964.

'Vysokaia trebovatel'nost''...(discussion of letters and the Lenin Prize), *Pravda*, April 11, 1964.

'Dobraia strogost'' (discussion of letters and the Lenin Prize), *Trud*, April 19, 1964.

Ivanov, I., 'Ne priukrashen li geroi?' (a letter on the work and the Lenin Prize), *Izvestiia*, December 29, 1963.

Marshak, S., 'Pravdivaia povest'', *Pravda*, January 30, 1964.

Pankov, V., 'Nositeli sveta', *Literaturnaia gazeta*, January 18, 1964.

Stavitskii, A., 'Za malym - mnogoe' (letter), *Literaturnaia gazeta*, January 23, 1964.

Note that *Pravda* announced the decisions of the Lenin Prize Committee on April 22, 1964. *One Day in the Life of Ivan Denisovich* was not mentioned.

Russian-language Articles Published in the West

Blagov, D. (pseud.), 'A. Solzhenitsyn i dukhovnaia missiia pisatelia', in *Sobranie sochinenii*, Possev, Frankfurt, 1969-70, vol. 6, pp. 287-355.

Gul', R., 'A. Solzhenitsyn, sotsrealizm i shkola Remizova', *Novyi zhurnal*, no. 71, 1963, pp. 58-74.

Lakshin, V., reprint of 'Ivan Denisovich, ego...' in *Sobranie sochinenii*, Possev, Frankfurt, 1969-70, vol. 6, pp. 243-86.

Rzhevskii, L., 'Obraz rasskazchika v povesti Solzhenitsyna "Odin den' Ivana Denisovicha"', in R. Magidoff et al (eds.), *Studies in Slavic Linguistics and Poetics in Honor of Boris O. Unbegaun*, New York University Press, New York, 1968, pp. 165-78.

Shiliaev, E., '"Lagernyi iazyk" po proizvedeniiam A.I. Solzhenitsyna', *Novyi zhurnal*, no. 95, 1969, pp. 232-247.

English-language Articles Published in the West

Bradley, T., 'Alexander Isaevich Solzhenitsyn', *Soviet Leaders* (ed. G. Simmonds), Crowell, New York, 1967, pp. 329-39.

Brown, E., 'Solzhenitsyn's Cast of Characters', *Slavic and East European Journal*, no. 2, 1971, pp. 153-66.

Erlich, V., 'Post-Stalin Trends in Russian Literature' and responses, *Slavic Review*, no. 3, 1964, pp. 405-19 and pp. 437-40.

Hayward, M., 'Solzhenitsyn's Place in Contemporary Soviet Literature', *Slavic Review*, no. 3, 1964, pp. 432-6.

Howe, I., 'Predicaments of Soviet Writing', *The New Republic*, May 11, 1963, pp. 19-21.

Kern, G., 'Solženicyn's Self-Censorship: The Canonical Text of *Odin Den' Ivana Denisoviča*', *Slavic and East European Journal*, vol. 20, no. 4, 1976, pp. 421-36.

———'Ivan the Worker', *Modern Fiction Studies*, 23, no. 1, 1977, pp. 5-30.

Luplow, R., 'Narrative Style and Structure in "One Day in the Life of Ivan Denisovich"', *Russian Literature Triquarterly*, no. 1, 1971, pp. 399-412.

Mihajlov, M., 'Dostoevsky's and Solzhenitsyn's "House of the Dead"',
    Russian Themes, Farrar, Straus and Giroux, New York, 1968, pp.
    78-118.
Monas, S., 'Ehrenburg's Life, Solzhenitsyn's Day', *Hudson Review*, no. 1,
    1963, pp. 112-21.
Perelmuter, J., 'Syntactical Aspects of Solženicyn's *Odin den' Ivana
    Denisoviča*', *Russian Language Journal*, 30, no. 105, (Winter 1976),
    pp. 8-24.
Pervushin, N., 'The Soviet Writer Solzhenitsyn, His Critics and the Classi-
    cal Russian Literature', *Slavic and East European Studies*, (Mont-
    real), nos. 1-2, 1965, pp. 3-19.
Pike, D., 'A Camp through the Eyes of a Peasant: Solzhenitsyn's *One Day
    in the Life of Ivan Denisovich*', *California Slavic Studies*, no. 10,
    1977, pp. 193-223.
Rus, V.J., '*One Day in the Life of Ivan Denisovich*: A Point of View
    Analysis', *Canadian Slavonic Papers*, 13, nos. 2-3, 1971, pp. 165-178.
Zekulin, G., 'Solzhenitsyn's Four Stories', *Soviet Studies*, no. 1, 1964, pp.
    45-62.

Books Containing Comment on *One Day in the Life of Ivan Denisovich*

Brown, D., *Soviet Russian Literature since Stalin*, Cambridge University
    Press, Cambridge and New York, 1978.
Brown, E., *Russian Literature since the Revolution*, Harvard University
    Press, Cambridge, Massachusetts, 1982.
Hayward, M., *Writers in Russia 1917-1978*, edited and with an Introduction
    by Patricia Blake, Collins/Harvill, London, 1983.
Hosking, G., *Beyond Socialist Realism: Soviet Fiction since Ivan Denisovich*,
    Paul Elek (Granada), London, 1980.
Slonim, M., *Soviet Russian Literature: Writers and Problems 1917-1977*,
    Second Revised Edition, Oxford University Press and New York,
    1977.

A forthcoming collection of essays specifically on *One Day in the Life of
Ivan Denisovich*, edited and introduced by Alexis Klimoff, is to be
published by Northwestern University Press.

Books specifically on Solzhenitsyn's Fiction

Allaback, S., *Alexander Solzhenitsyn*, Taplinger, New York, 1978.
Kodjak, A., *Alexander Solzhenitsyn*, Twayne, Boston, 1978.
Lukács, G., *Solzhenitsyn*, translated by William Graf, Merlin Press, London,
    1969.
Moody, C., *Solzhenitsyn*, Oliver and Boyd, Edinburgh, second revised edition,
    1976.

Rothberg, A., *Aleksandr Solzhenitsyn: The Major Novels*, Ithaca, Cornell University Press, 1971.

Rzhevskii, L., *Solzhenitsyn: Creator and Heroic Deed*, University of Alabama Press, 1978.

Index

Trotsky, L., 45, 102
truth, 3-5, 29-30, 31, 34, 37, 43, 47, 56, 58
Tsezar, Markovich, 21, 24, 36, 63, 69, 78, 80, 84, 88, 93, 94 ff.,
Turgenev, I., 96
Turkin, V., 96
Tvardovsky, A., 9-16 *passim*, 20-1, 29-31, 51-2, 68, 97, 107
Tyurin (also Tiurin), Andrei Prokofievich, 16, 21, 28, 69-73, 75, 78, 84, 90, 91 ff., 98
Ukrainians, 21, 24
Ulysses, 64
Union of Soviet Writers, 8, 9, 10, 12, 42, 43, 102
Ust'-Izhma, 63, 71, 86, 87
Valéry, P., 58
Vdovushkin, 61, 74, 95, 96
'village prose', 85, 90

Vinokur, T., 37, 38, 39, 40, 53, 107
Virgil, 70
Vitkevich, N., 10
Voinovich, V., 15
Volkovoi, 62, 73, 84, 90, 92
Voznesensky, A., 9
Vyatka, 69, 70
Williams, C., 19
Yarkevich, I., 4
Yeats, W., 58
Yermolaev, 69
Yu-81, 23, 32, 80
Zakhar Vasilievich, 70
Zamyatin, E., 26, 58, 65-6
Zavadsky, Yu., v, 97, 101
zek, 7, 25, 72, 74, 76, 77, 81, 90, 92, 93, 94
Zekulin, G., 40, 41, 42, 53, 109
Zhukov, G., 9
Znamya, 14